Scott Foresman
Science

See learning in a whole new light

PEARSON
Scott Foresman

Editorial Offices: Glenview, Illinois • Parsippany, New Jersey • New York, New York
Sales Offices: Boston, Massachusetts • Duluth, Georgia • Glenview, Illinois
Coppell, Texas • Sacramento, California • Mesa, Arizona

Series Authors

Dr. Timothy Cooney
*Professor of Earth Science and
Science Education*
University of Northern Iowa (UNI)
Cedar Falls, Iowa

Dr. Jim Cummins
Professor
Department of Curriculum,
Teaching, and Learning
University of Toronto
Toronto, Canada

Dr. James Flood
*Distinguished Professor of Literacy
and Language*
School of Teacher Education
San Diego State University
San Diego, California

Barbara Kay Foots, M.Ed.
Science Education Consultant
Houston, Texas

Dr. M. Jenice Goldston
*Associate Professor of Science
Education*
Department of Elementary
Education Programs
University of Alabama
Tuscaloosa, Alabama

Dr. Shirley Gholston Key
*Associate Professor of Science
Education*
Instruction and Curriculum
Leadership Department
College of Education
University of Memphis
Memphis, Tennessee

Dr. Diane Lapp
*Distinguished Professor of Reading
and Language Arts in Teacher
Education*
San Diego State University
San Diego, California

Sheryl A. Mercier
Classroom Teacher
Dunlap Elementary School
Dunlap, California

Dr. Karen L. Ostlund
Director
UTeach, College of Natural
Sciences
The University of Texas at Austin
Austin, Texas

Dr. Nancy Romance
*Professor of Science Education
& Principal Investigator*
NSF/IERI Science IDEAS Project
Charles E. Schmidt College of
Science
Florida Atlantic University
Boca Raton, Florida

Dr. William Tate
*Chair and Professor of Education
and Applied Statistics*
Department of Education
Washington University
St. Louis, Missouri

Dr. Kathryn C. Thornton
Professor
School of Engineering and
Applied Science
University of Virginia
Charlottesville, Virginia

Dr. Leon Ukens
Professor of Science Education
Department of Physics,
Astronomy, and Geosciences
Towson University
Towson, Maryland

Steve Weinberg
Consultant
Connecticut Center for
Advanced Technology
East Hartford, Connecticut

ISBN: 0-328-10001-3 (SVE); ISBN: 0-328-15671-X (A); ISBN: 0-328-15677-9 (B);
ISBN: 0-328-15683-3 (C); ISBN: 0-328-15689-2 (D)

8 9 10 V063 12 11 10 09 08 07

Consulting Author

Dr. Michael P. Klentschy
Superintendent
El Centro Elementary School District
El Centro, California

Science Content Consultants

Dr. Frederick W. Taylor
Senior Research Scientist
Institute for Geophysics
Jackson School of Geosciences
The University of Texas at Austin
Austin, Texas

Dr. Ruth E. Buskirk
Senior Lecturer
School of Biological Sciences
The University of Texas at Austin
Austin, Texas

Dr. Cliff Frohlich
Senior Research Scientist
Institute for Geophysics
Jackson School of Geosciences
The University of Texas at Austin
Austin, Texas

Brad Armosky
McDonald Observatory
The University of Texas at Austin
Austin, Texas

NASA Content Consultants

Adena Williams Loston, Ph.D.
Chief Education Officer
Office of the Chief Education Officer

Clifford W. Houston, Ph.D.
Deputy Chief Education Officer for Education Programs
Office of the Chief Education Officer

Frank C. Owens
Senior Policy Advisor
Office of the Chief Education Officer

Deborah Brown Biggs
Manager, Education Flight Projects Office
Space Operations Mission Directorate, Education Lead

Erika G. Vick
NASA Liaison to Pearson Scott Foresman
Education Flight Projects Office

William E. Anderson
Partnership Manager for Education
Aeronautics Research Mission Directorate

Anita Krishnamurthi
Program Planning Specialist
Space Science Education and Outreach Program

Bonnie J. McClain
Chief of Education
Exploration Systems Mission Directorate

Diane Clayton, Ph.D.
Program Scientist
Earth Science Education

Deborah Rivera
Strategic Alliances Manager
Office of Public Affairs
NASA Headquarters

Douglas D. Peterson
Public Affairs Officer, Astronaut Office
Office of Public Affairs
NASA Johnson Space Center

Nicole Cloutier
Public Affairs Officer, Astronaut Office
Office of Public Affairs
NASA Johnson Space Center

Dr. Jennifer J. Wiseman
Hubble Space Telescope Program Scientist
NASA Headquarters

Reviewers

Science

See learning in a whole new light

Unit A Life Science

What do living things need?

Chapter 1 • Living and Nonliving

Chapter 2 • Habitats

Where do plants and animals live?

Unit A Life Science

How do parts help living things?

Chapter 3 • How Plants and Animals Live

Chapter 4 • Life Cycles

How do animals and plants grow and change?

Unit A Life Science

How are living things connected?

Chapter 5 • Food Chains

Unit B Earth Science

How are land, water, and air important?

WE RECYCLE

Chapter 7 • Weather

What are the four seasons?

Unit C Physical Science

How can objects be described?

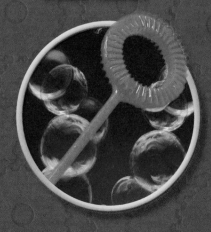

Chapter 8 • Observing Matter

Chapter 9 • Movement and Sound

What makes objects move?

Unit C Physical Science

Where does energy come from?

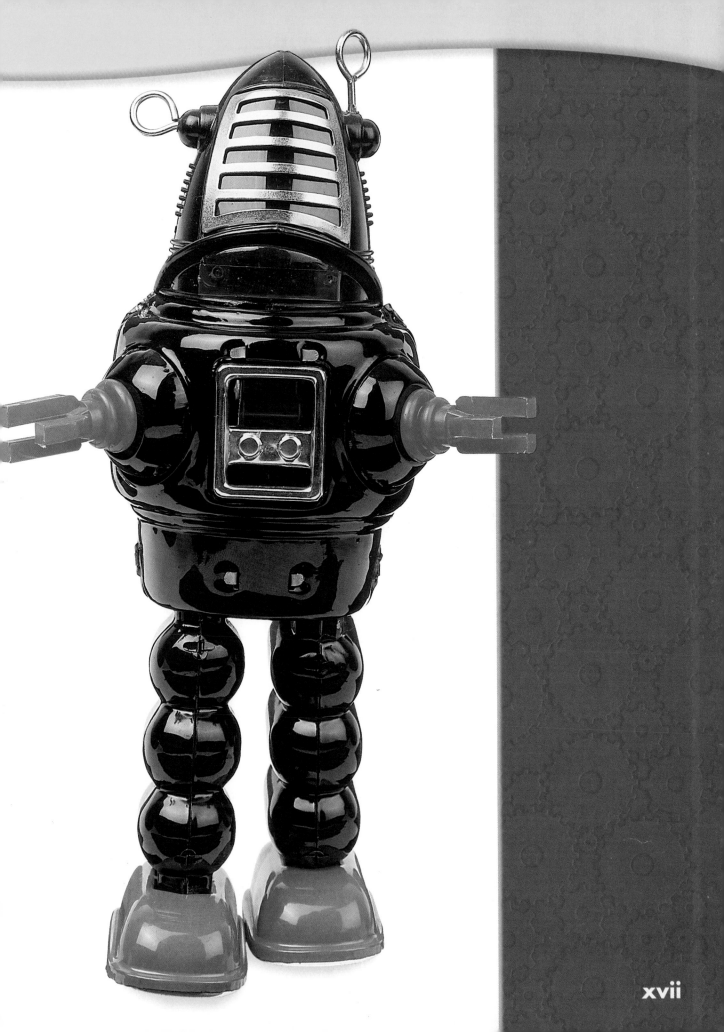

Unit D Space and Technology

What is in the sky?

Chapter 12 • Science in Our World

How does technology help people?

Science Process Skills

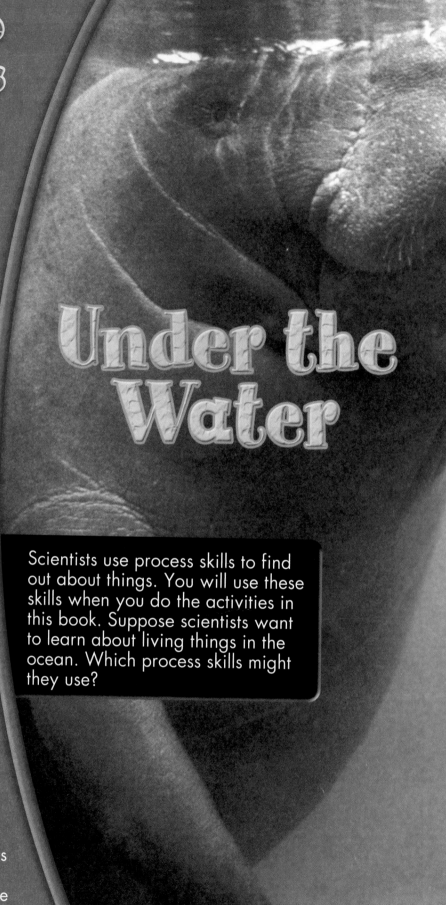

Observe

A scientist who wants to find out about the ocean observes many things. You use your senses to find out about things too.

Classify

Scientists classify living things in the ocean. You classify when you sort or group things by their properties.

Estimate and Measure

Scientists can estimate the size of living things in the ocean. This means they make a careful guess about the size or amount of something. Then they measure it.

Infer

Scientists are always learning about living things in the ocean. Scientists draw a conclusion or make a guess from what they already know.

Under the Water

Scientists use process skills to find out about things. You will use these skills when you do the activities in this book. Suppose scientists want to learn about living things in the ocean. Which process skills might they use?

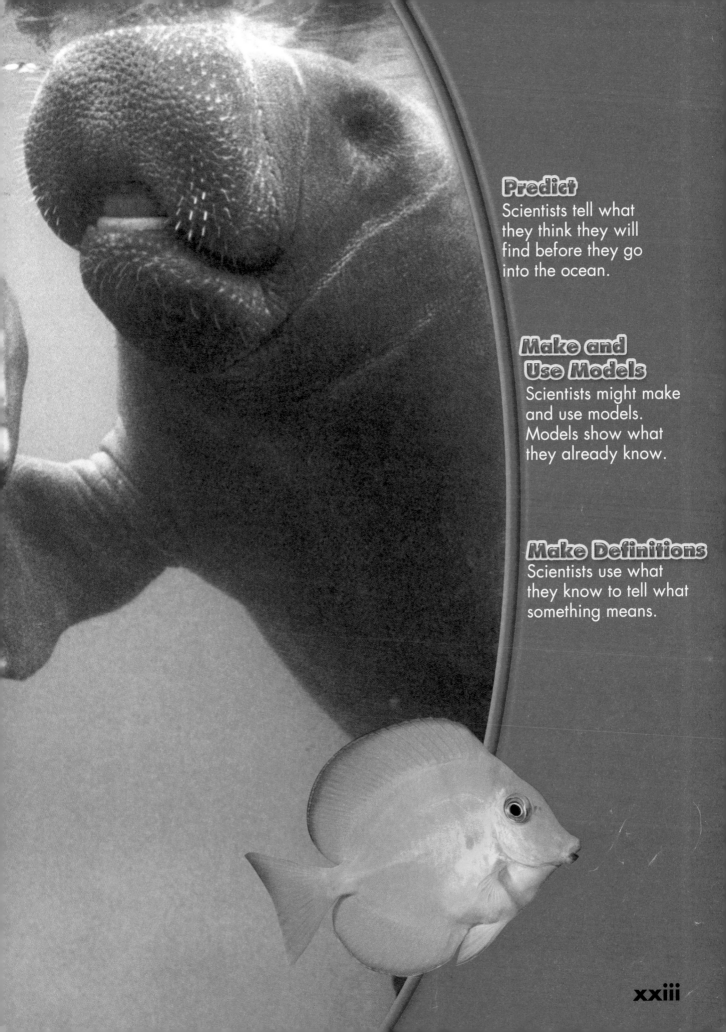

Predict
Scientists tell what they think they will find before they go into the ocean.

Make and Use Models
Scientists might make and use models. Models show what they already know.

Make Definitions
Scientists use what they know to tell what something means.

Science Process Skills

Make Hypotheses

Think of a question you have about living things in the ocean. Make a statement that you can test to answer your question.

Collect Data

Scientists record what they observe and measure. Scientists put this data into charts or graphs.

Interpret Data

Scientists use what they learn to solve problems or answer questions.

Suppose you were a scientist. You might want to learn more about the ocean. What questions might you have? How would you use process skills to help you learn?

Investigate and Experiment
Scientists plan and do an investigation as they study the ocean.

Control Variables
Scientists plan a fair test. Scientists change only one thing in their test. Scientists keep everything else the same.

Communicate
Scientists tell what they learn about living things in the ocean.

Using Scientific Methods

Scientific methods are ways of finding answers. Scientific methods have these steps. Sometimes scientists do the steps in a different order. Scientists do not always do all of the steps.

Ask a question.

Ask a question that you want answered.

Do seeds need water to grow?

Make your hypothesis.

Tell what you think the answer is to your question.

If seeds are watered, then they will grow.

Plan a fair test.

Change only one thing.

Keep everything else the same.

Water one pot with seeds.

water

no water

Do your test.

Test your hypothesis. Do your test more than once. See if your results are the same.

Collect and record your data.

Keep records of what you find out. Use words or drawings to help.

Tell your conclusion.

Observe the results of your test. Decide if your hypothesis is right or wrong. Tell what you decide.

Seeds need water to grow.

no water

water

Go further.

Use what you learn. Think of new questions or better ways to do a test.

Ask a Question

Make Your Hypothesis

Plan a Fair Test

Do Your Test

Collect and Record Your Data

Tell Your Conclusion

Go Further

Science Tools

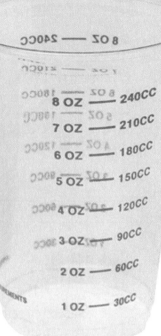

Scientists use many different kinds of tools.

Measuring cup
You can use a measuring cup to measure volume. Volume is how much space something takes up.

Stopwatch
A stopwatch measures how much time something takes.

Computer
You can learn about science at a special Internet website. Go to www.sfsuccessnet.com.

Ruler
You can use a ruler to measure how long something is. Most scientists use a ruler to measure length in centimeters or millimeters.

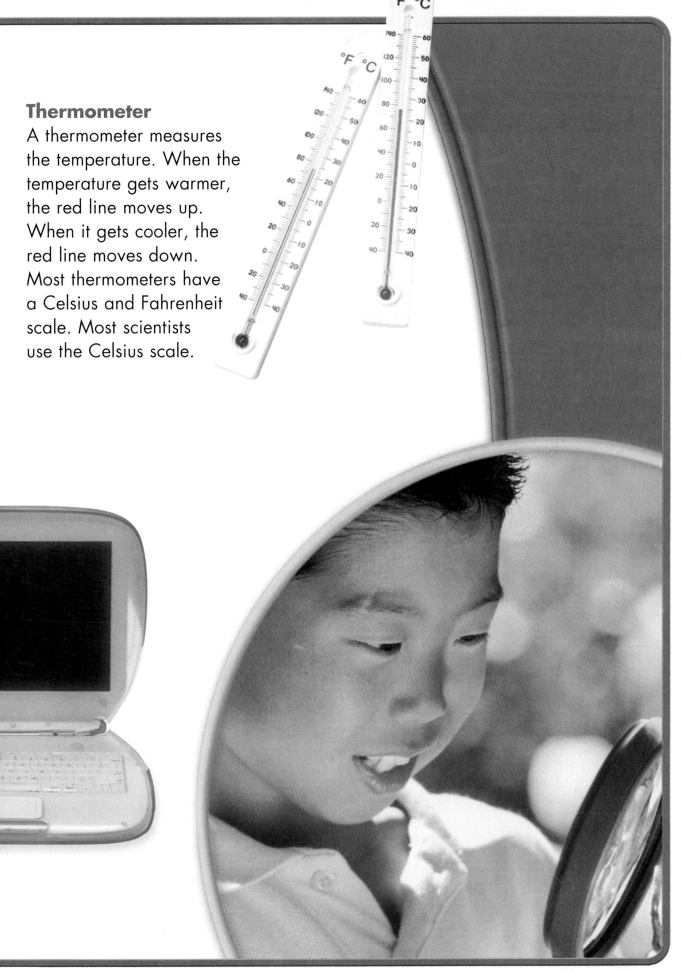

Thermometer

A thermometer measures the temperature. When the temperature gets warmer, the red line moves up. When it gets cooler, the red line moves down. Most thermometers have a Celsius and Fahrenheit scale. Most scientists use the Celsius scale.

Science Tools

Safety goggles
You can use safety goggles to protect your eyes.

Calculator
A calculator can help you do things, such as add and subtract.

Balance
A balance is used to measure the mass of objects. Mass is how much matter an object has. Most scientists measure mass in grams or kilograms.

Meterstick
You can use a meterstick to measure how long something is too. Scientists use a meterstick to measure in meters.

Clock
A clock measures time.

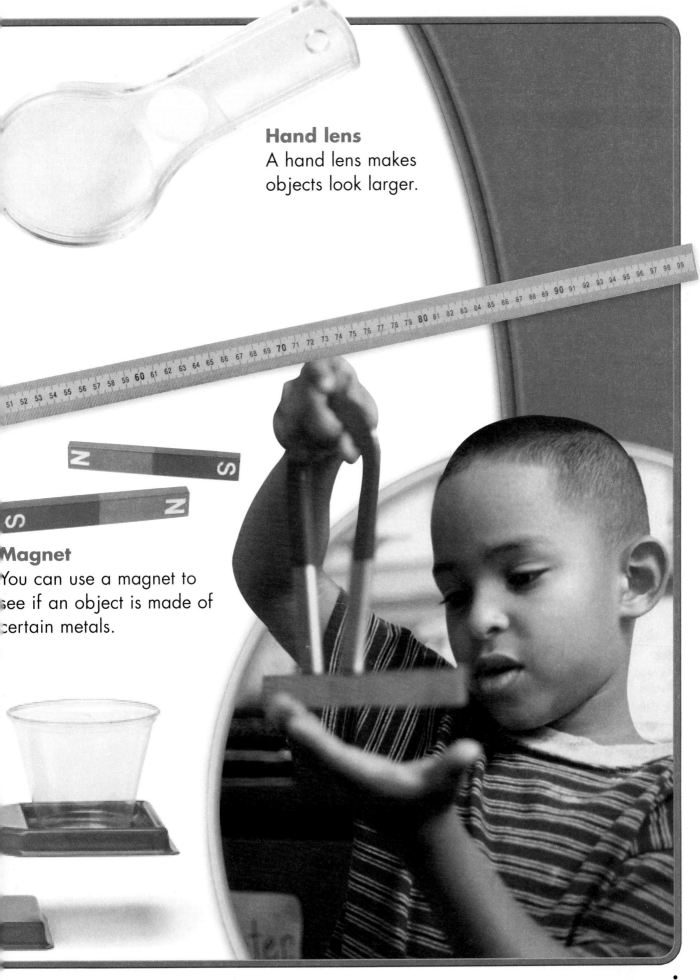

Hand lens
A hand lens makes objects look larger.

Magnet
You can use a magnet to see if an object is made of certain metals.

Safety in Science

You need to be careful when doing science activities. This page includes safety tips to remember:

- Listen to your teacher's instructions.
- Never taste or smell materials unless your teacher tells you to.
- Wear safety goggles when needed.
- Handle scissors and other equipment carefully.
- Keep your work place neat and clean.
- Clean up spills immediately.
- Tell your teacher immediately about accidents or if you see something that looks unsafe.
- Wash your hands well after every activity.

Unit A

Life Science

Chapter 1
Living and Nonliving

You Will Discover

- why living things are alive.
- that nonliving things were never alive.

online
Student Edition
sfsuccessnet.com

What do living things need?

living

shelter

2

Chapter 1
Vocabulary
....

nonliving

Explore Which is a living thing?

Materials

bowl with gravel

bean seeds

cup with water

What to Do

1 Put the bean seeds on the gravel.

2 Cover the gravel with water. Observe for 4 days.

Process Skills

You **observe** when you watch the seeds and the gravel.

Explain Your Results
Observe what happens.
Tell about the changes you see.

How to Read Science

TARGET SKILL

Alike and Different

Alike means how things are the same. Different means how things are not the same.

Science Pictures

Apply It!

Observe the trees. How are the trees alike and different?

Alike	Different

5

Is it Living?
I'd Like to Know!

Sung to the tune of "Clementine."
Lyrics by Gerri Brioso & Richard Freitas/The Dovetail Group, Inc.

Plants are living things.

So are animals.

So are people, and I know,

Living things need food and water.

Living things all change and grow.

Lesson 1

What are living things?

Living things are alive.
Living things can grow.
Living things can change.

Plants are living things.
Animals are living things.
People are living things too.

This butterfly is a living thing.

Plants and Animals

Plants can grow.
Plants can change.

**This young oak
tree will grow.**

Animals can grow.
Animals can change.

Grown animals can
have young animals.

Many animals can
move on their own.

How do these animals move?

✓ **Lesson Checkpoint**

1. What is a living thing?

2. **Math** in Science What could you use to measure how tall the young oak tree is?

9

What do plants need?

A need is something a living thing must have to live.

Plants need air and water.
Plants need light from the Sun.
Plants need space to live and grow.

Rain can give plants the water they need.

✔Lesson Checkpoint

1. What do plants need to live?

2. Writing in Science Tell how plants can get water.

What do animals need?

Animals have needs too.
Animals need food.
Animals need water.
Animals need air.

Animals need space to live.
Some animals need shelter.
A **shelter** is a safe place.

Munch!
The chipmunk eats flower parts for food.

The birds use a nest for shelter. This nest is made of sticks and grasses.

What does this wolf pup use for shelter?

✓ **Lesson Checkpoint**

1. What do animals need to live?

2. 🔄 How are the needs of plants and animals **alike and different**?

13

Lesson 4

What are nonliving things?

Nonliving things were never alive.
Nonliving things do not need
food and water.

Nonliving things do not grow
on their own.
Nonliving things do not change
on their own.

1. ✓**Checkpoint** How do you know that
a chair is a nonliving thing?

2. **Writing** in Science Draw a picture of
a nonliving thing. Write one sentence
about your picture.

Look at the classroom.
What nonliving things
do you see?

Nonliving Things Around You

People make some nonliving things. People make some toys that look like living things. People make some toys that move like living things.

Name some nonliving things in the bathtub.

There are nonliving things in nature.
Water is a nonliving thing.
Water does not need food.
Water does not grow.

What nonliving things do you see in this picture?

✓ **Lesson Checkpoint**

1. What are some nonliving things made by people?

2. 🎯 How are a toy dog and a living dog **alike and different**?

Investigate How do brine shrimp eggs change in salt water?

Materials

spoon with
shrimp eggs

hand lens

cup with salt water

What to Do

1 Look at the shrimp eggs with a hand lens. Draw a picture to show how they look.

2 Add the shrimp eggs to the salt water.

Process Skills

You **interpret data** when you use data to answer questions.

More Lab zone Activities Take It to the Net
sfsuccessnet.com

3 Observe the eggs for 5 days.

4 **Collect Data** Draw a picture each day to show what happens to the shrimp eggs.

Observing Brine Shrimp				
Day 1	Day 2	Day 3	Day 4	Day 5

Explain Your Results

1. **Interpret Data** What changes did you observe in 5 days?

2. What do brine shrimp eggs need to grow and change?

Go Further

Could shrimp eggs live in water that is not salty? How could you find out?

Sorting and Counting
Living and Nonliving Things

Find living and nonliving things in the picture.

Count the living things. Write the number.

Count the nonliving things. Write the number.

Living Things	Nonliving Things

Lab zone **Take-Home Activity**

Look around your home. List three living things you see. List three nonliving things you see.

Vocabulary

Which picture goes with each word?

1. living
2. nonliving

What did you learn?

3. What do plants need to live?

4. What do animals need to live?

5. What might happen if a living thing does not get what it needs?

6. Observe Tell two things about a nonliving object you see in your classroom?

Alike and Different

7. How are these birds **alike and different**?

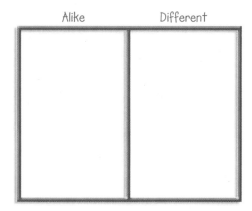

Alike	Different

Test Prep

Fill in the circle next to the correct answer.

8. Which one is nonliving?

Ⓐ a person

Ⓑ a hat

Ⓒ a dog

Ⓓ a plant

9. Writing in Science Make a list of three things you need to live.

Dr. Sonia Ortega

Dr. Ortega is a marine biologist.

Read Together

Dr. Sonia Ortega liked to look for insects when she was young. When she grew up she wanted to learn more about other animals.

Now Dr. Ortega studies oysters in the Atlantic Ocean. She wants to know where oysters grow the best.

Lab zone Take-Home Activity

Look for animals near your home. Draw pictures of them.

EC NTL 10 9 8 7 6 5 4

Chapter 2
Habitats

You Will Discover

- how habitats are alike and different.

- how the needs of plants and animals are met in their habitats.

Discovery Channel School
Student DVD
DISCOVERY CHANNEL SCHOOL

online
Student Edition
sfsuccessnet.com

Where do plants and animals live?

habitat

forest

wetland

26

Chapter 2
Vocabulary

ocean

desert

27

Explore Where do animals live?

Materials

yarn

picture cards

word cards

What to Do

1 Make 2 yarn circles.

2 Sort the picture cards.
Which animals live on land?
Which animals live in water?

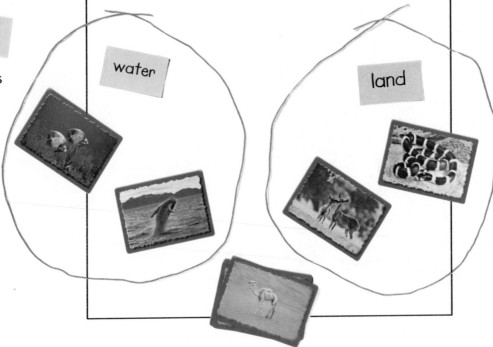

Process Skills

Sorting things is a way to show what you **observe**.

Explain Your Results
Observe the 2 groups.
Tell where each animal lives.

Reading Skills

Picture Clues

Pictures can give you clues about what you read.

Science Story

Grassland

These animals live in a grassland. The animals gather at the waterhole. The animals need water to live.

giraffe

grassland

Apply It!

Observe What lives in this grassland? Look for clues in the picture.

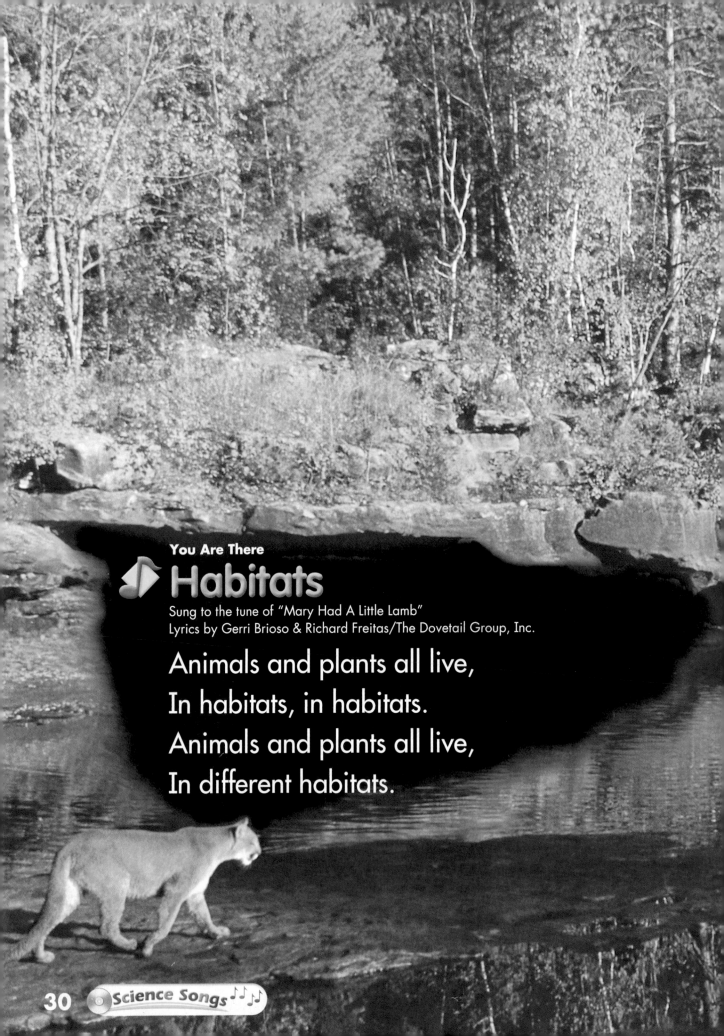

You Are There

🎵 Habitats

Sung to the tune of "Mary Had A Little Lamb"
Lyrics by Gerri Brioso & Richard Freitas/The Dovetail Group, Inc.

Animals and plants all live,

In habitats, in habitats.

Animals and plants all live,

In different habitats.

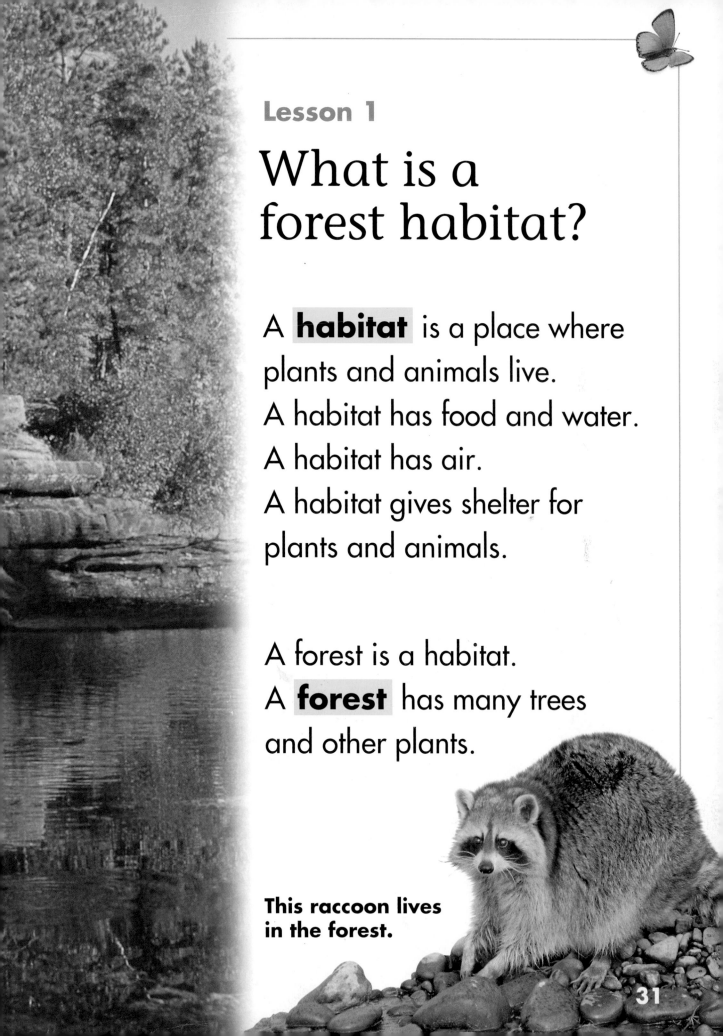

Lesson 1

What is a forest habitat?

A **habitat** is a place where plants and animals live.
A habitat has food and water.
A habitat has air.
A habitat gives shelter for plants and animals.

A forest is a habitat.
A **forest** has many trees and other plants.

This raccoon lives in the forest.

Forest Plants and Animals

Look at the forest
in the summer.

Animals get the food
they need. Animals
get the water they need.

Plants get the sunlight
they need. Plants get
the water they need.

**This black bear lives
in the forest.**

32

winter

Look at the forest in the winter.

How does the forest change?

Plants get less sunlight. Many trees lose their leaves. It is harder for some animals to find food.

Map Facts
Superior National Forest is in Minnesota.

✓ **Lesson Checkpoint**

1. What is a habitat?

2. Use **picture clues** to tell how the forest changes.

33

What is a wetland habitat?

A **wetland** habitat is covered with water.
A wetland has food and water for animals.
A wetland has shelter for animals.

Look at this picture of a wetland.
Plants in this wetland get sunlight.
This wetland gets lots of rain in the summer.
This wetland gets less rain in the winter.
The winter is cooler than the summer.

This duck lives in a wetland.

Map Facts
A swamp is a wetland. Okefenokee Swamp in Georgia has about 70 islands.

crane

dragonfly

bullfrog

✓ **Lesson Checkpoint**

1. What does a duck get in a wetland?

2. 🔄 Use **picture clues** to tell what animals live in a wetland.

35

What is an ocean habitat?

An **ocean** is a habitat.
An ocean has salt water.
An ocean is large and deep.

Many plants and animals live in an ocean.

Plants and animals get everything they need to live in their ocean habitat.

√ **Lesson Checkpoint**

1. What is an ocean?

2. **Writing** in Science Write in your **science journal.** Write a sentence about living things in an ocean.

sea turtle

whale

fish

What is a desert habitat?

A **desert** is a habitat.
A desert is very dry.
A desert gets lots of sunlight.
A desert gets very little rain.
Many deserts are hot during the day.

Many animals and plants live
in the desert. The camel can live
without water for a long time.
The cactus can store water in its stems.

This fennec fox stays underground during the hot desert day.

Map Facts

The Sahara Desert is the largest desert in the world.

Africa

United States Desert

✓ **Lesson Checkpoint**

1. What is a desert?

2. **Math** in Science Which thermometer shows the temperature of a desert during the hot day?

A

B

39

Investigate How do desert leaves hold water?

Materials

desert leaf shapes

water

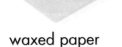

waxed paper

What to Do

1 Wet the leaf shapes.

2 Fold the waxed paper over one leaf shape.

The waxed paper is like a waxy cover on a desert leaf.

3 Put both leaf shapes in a sunny place.

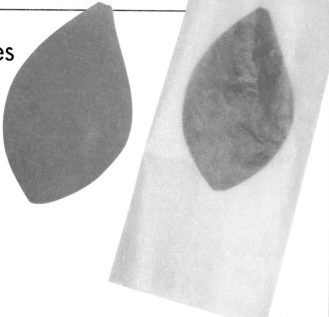

4 **Predict** Which leaf shape holds water longer?

	Predict	What happens?

Explain Your Results
Infer Why might a desert leaf have a waxy covering?

Go Further
What other question do you have about leaves? Plan a test to find the answer.

Counting Animals

forest

desert

Make a tally chart.
Count the animals in the forest picture.
Count the animals in the desert picture.

forest	desert

Which of these pictures shows more animals?

Lab zone **Take-Home Activity**

Draw plants and animals in a habitat. Are there more plants or animals? Share your picture with your family.

Vocabulary

Which picture goes with each word?

1. desert

2. forest

3. ocean

4. wetland

What did you learn?

5. What do these plants get from their habitat?

6. What does this deer get from its habitat?

7. Observe Describe a habitat near your school. What plants and animals live there?

Picture Clues

8. Use **picture clues** to tell about the wetland.

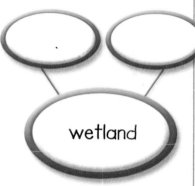

wetland

Test Prep

Fill in the circle next to the correct answer.

9. In which habitat might you see a camel?
- Ⓐ desert
- Ⓑ ocean
- Ⓒ rain forest
- Ⓓ wetland

10. Writing in Science Tell how a forest and a desert are alike and different.

45

Habitats at Kennedy Space Center

Kennedy Space Center is on Merritt Island. Kennedy Space Center is part of a wildlife refuge. A wildlife refuge keeps animals safe. This refuge has many habitats.

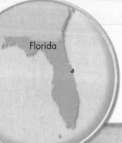

Florida

Map Facts
Merritt Island is in Florida.

Bald Eagles

Bald eagle nests on the wildlife refuge are safe.

Sea Turtles

Sea turtles lay their eggs on land. Their eggs are safe on the refuge.

Manatees

Manatees swim in the Banana River on the refuge. They are safe here.

Lab zone Take-Home Activity

Draw a picture of an animal that lives on Merritt Island. Tell your family about the animal.

Naturalists

Read Together

Naturalists study animals and plants.
Some naturalists help young cranes.
Some naturalists lead young cranes
to their winter habitat in Florida.
Now the cranes will know
where to go each winter.

This naturalist is leading cranes from Wisconsin to Florida.

Lab zone Take-Home Activity

Find Wisconsin and Florida
on a United States map. Tell
your family how naturalists
help young cranes.

EC NTL 10 9 8 7 6 5 4

You Will Discover

- parts that help plants and animals live in their habitats.
- parts that help living things keep safe.

Chapter 3
How Plants and Animals Live

online
Student Edition
sfsuccessnet.com

How do parts help living things?

flower

antennae

camouflage

Chapter 3 Vocabulary

root

stem

leaf

Explore How can fur keep animals warm?

Materials

2 thermometers

2 plastic bags

cotton balls

tub with ice water

What to Do

1 Read the thermometers.

2 Put a thermometer in each bag. Add cotton balls to one bag.

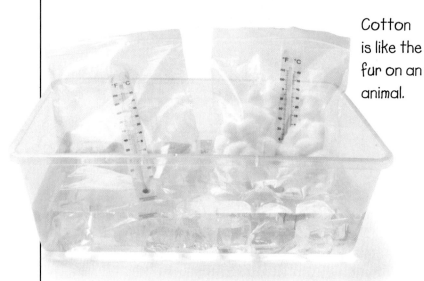

Cotton is like the fur on an animal.

3 Put the bags in ice water for 1 minute. **Predict** what will happen to each thermometer. Read the thermometers.

Explain Your Results

Communicate Tell how the thermometers show that fur can keep an animal warm.

How to Read Science

 Alike and Different

Alike means how things are the same. Different means how things are not the same.

Science Pictures

Apply It!

Communicate

Tell how the foxes are alike and different.

Alike	Different

53

Something Special

Sung to the tune of "Froggie Went A Courtin'"
Lyrics by Gerri Brioso & Richard Freitas/The Dovetail Group, Inc.

It's very cold where the
  mountain goat lives, ah hmm.
It's very cold where the
  mountain goat lives, ah hmm.
But he has thick fur to keep him warm,
Even if there's a big snowstorm.
Ah hmm. Ah hmm. Ah hmm.

Lesson 1

What helps animals live in their habitats?

Some animal body parts help animals live in their habitats.

These mountain goats live in a cold habitat. Thick fur helps keep the goats warm.

Hooves

Hooves help the goats climb on the rocks.

Living in the Ocean

This hermit crab lives in the ocean.
This hermit crab lives in a shell.
The hard shell helps keep the
hermit crab safe.

A hermit crab has antennae.
Antennae are feelers.
Antennae help the crab feel,
smell, and taste.

Antennae

The hermit crab
grew out of its
shell. Another
animal left its
shell. The hermit
crab moved in!

Swish! The clownfish uses fins to swim quickly in the ocean.

The clownfish uses a sea anemone for shelter.
A sea anemone is an animal.

☑ **Lesson Checkpoint**

1. What helps keep mountain goats warm?

2. **Writing** in Science Write a sentence about a hermit crab's home.

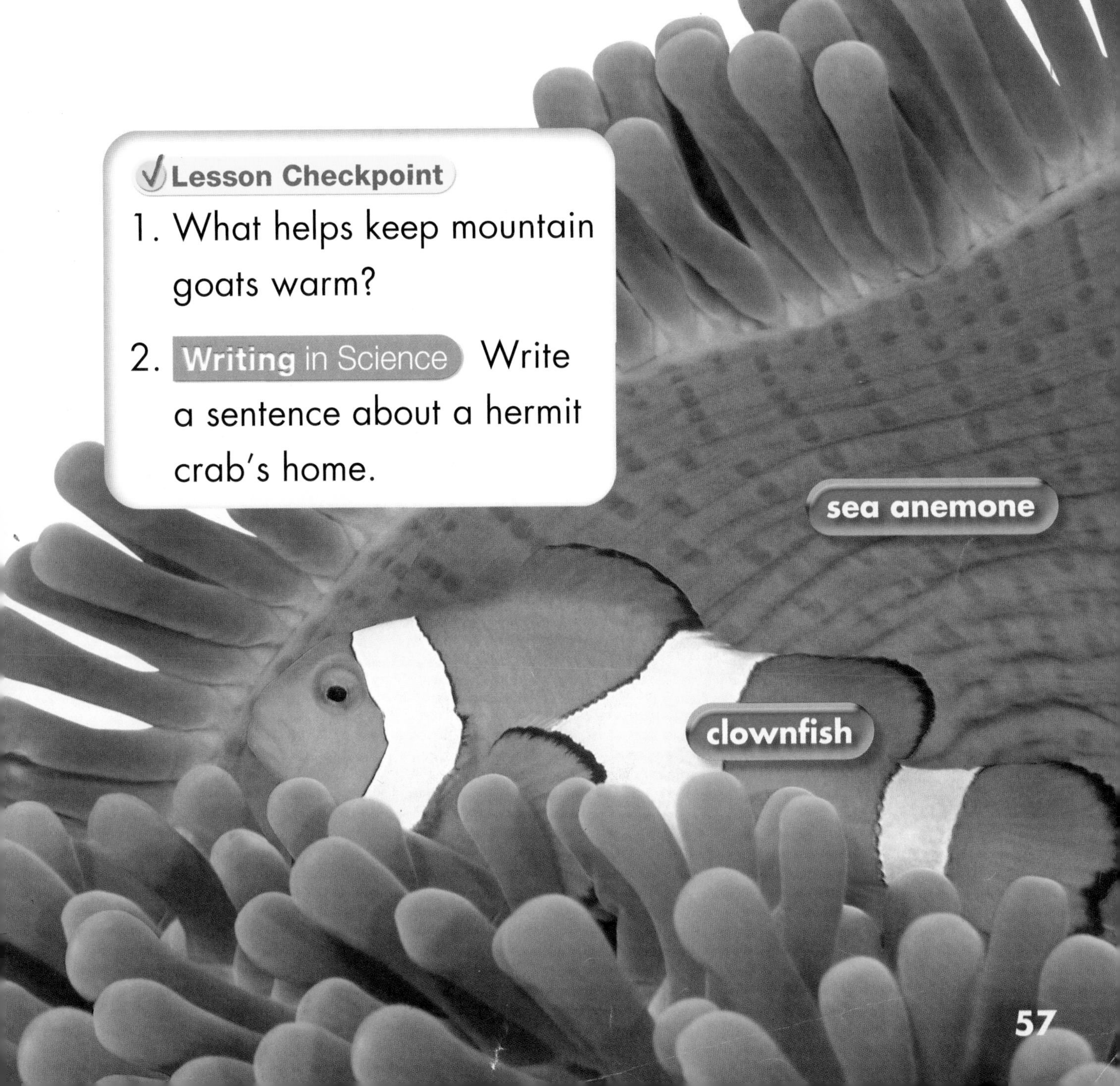

sea anemone

clownfish

How do animals get food?

Animals use parts of their body to get food.

Birds fly to find food.
Birds use wings and feathers to fly.

Birds use beaks to eat food.
Crack! The cardinal's beak breaks seeds.
The owl's sharp beak tears meat.

Owl

Cardinal

Camels live in some deserts.
Food and water can be hard
to find in the desert.

A camel's hump has fat.
The fat helps the camel
live without food and
water for a long time.

1. ✔Checkpoint What part of a
   camel helps it live in a desert?

2. 🎯 How are bird beaks
   alike and different?

Other Ways Animals Get Food

Whoosh! See the lion run. Strong legs help the lion run quickly.

The lion has good eyesight. The lion uses its nose to smell food. The lion's whiskers help it feel things.

A lion has long, sharp teeth for eating.

A lion catches animals with its claws.

The lion tries to catch the zebra.

Look at the giraffes.
Giraffes have long necks.
Giraffes can reach
the leaves high in the tree.
Giraffes chew the leaves
with their flat teeth.

Giraffes eat leaves.

✓**Lesson Checkpoint**

1. What body parts help the lion catch food?

2. 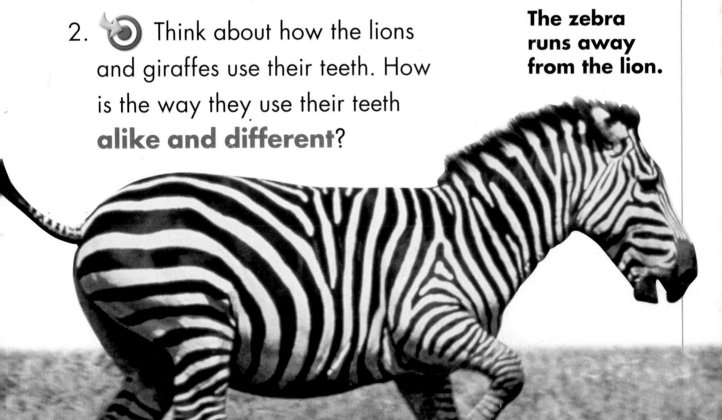 Think about how the lions and giraffes use their teeth. How is the way they use their teeth **alike and different**?

The zebra runs away from the lion.

What can help protect animals?

Camouflage is a color or shape. Camouflage makes an animal or plant hard to see.

Look at the snowshoe hares. Camouflage helps protect snowshoe hares.

The hare's fur is brown. The hare is hard to see in the woods.

The hare's fur changes to white. The hare is hard to see in the snow.

Can you find the katydid? Camouflage helps keep the katydid safe.

The katydid uses its antennae to find its way in the dark.

Earthworms live underground where they are away from the light. Heat and light dry out worms.

1. ✅ Checkpoint How does the hare stay safe?

2. 🔄 How are the katydid and the hare **alike and different**?

63

Hiding in the Water

The crocodile lives in the water.
The hippopotamus lives in the water.

The crocodile and the hippopotamus
swim with only their eyes above the water.
It is hard for other animals to see them.

Crocodiles open
their eyes under
water. Special lids
keep their eyes
safe.

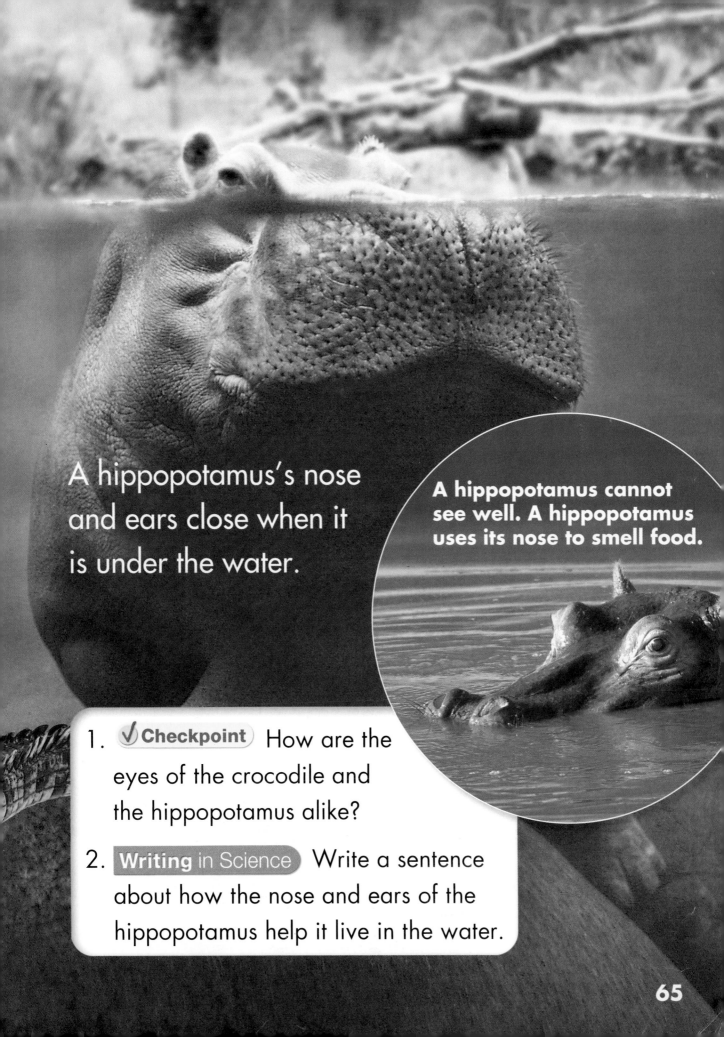

A hippopotamus's nose and ears close when it is under the water.

A hippopotamus cannot see well. A hippopotamus uses its nose to smell food.

1. ✓Checkpoint How are the eyes of the crocodile and the hippopotamus alike?

2. Writing in Science Write a sentence about how the nose and ears of the hippopotamus help it live in the water.

Animals Warn of Danger

Danger is near. This deer lifts and waves its white tail. Other deer see this and run.

Kangaroos move their ears to hear sounds all around.

Thump! Danger is near. The kangaroo pounds the ground with its back legs. Other kangaroos hear this and jump away.

A peacock's loud call can mean danger is near.

Screech! Danger is near. The peacock makes a very loud call. Other peacocks know to hide.

✓Lesson Checkpoint

1. How do deer warn each other of danger?

2. **Technology** in Science What sounds warn people of danger?

Lesson 4

What are some parts of plants?

You learned about parts of animals. What parts of plants help them live and grow?

The **root** takes in water. Roots hold the plant in the ground. The **stem** takes water from the roots. Stems carry water to parts of the plant.

This stem's sharp thorns keep hungry animals away.

Roots

Stem

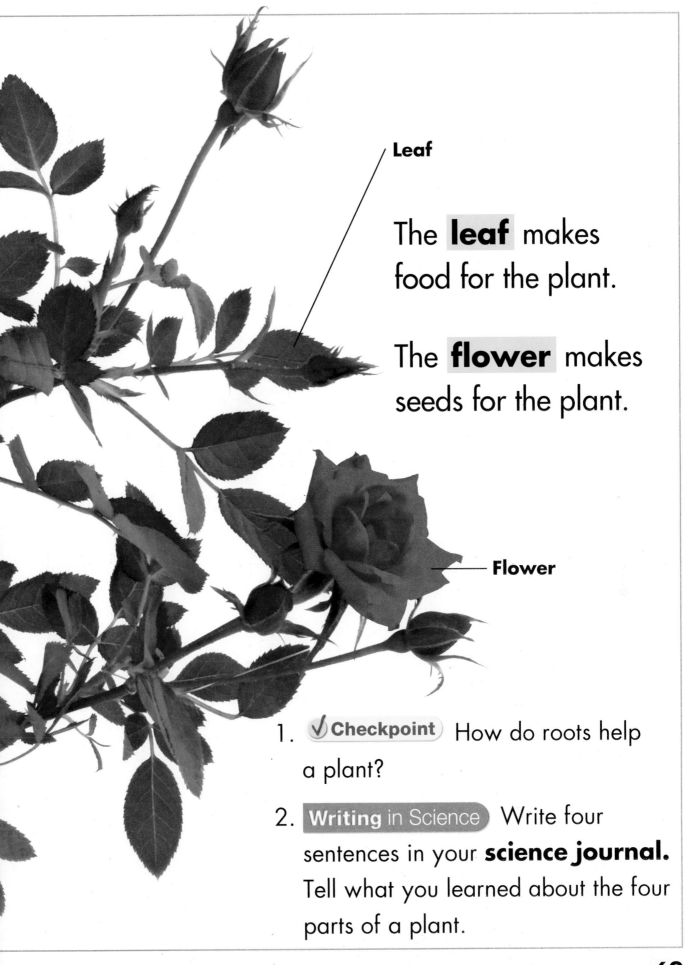

Leaf

The **leaf** makes food for the plant.

The **flower** makes seeds for the plant.

Flower

1. ✓ **Checkpoint** How do roots help a plant?

2. **Writing** in Science Write four sentences in your **science journal.** Tell what you learned about the four parts of a plant.

Plants in Different Habitats

Look at the pictures.
These plants grow in different habitats.
These plants have different kinds
of leaves. The leaves have different
shapes and sizes.

Rain slides off this pointy leaf. This shape helps the leaf stay dry.

Wetland

Needles stay on the pine tree in winter. Needles help the pine tree hold water.

Forest

The sizes and shapes of leaves help plants live and grow.

✓ **Lesson Checkpoint**

1. What part helps the cactus live in the desert?

2. 🎯 How are the leaves of these plants **alike and different**?

Spines keep this cactus from losing water in the dry desert. Spines are leaves that look like needles.

Desert

Parts of the rain forest do not get much sunlight. Big leaves can take in more sunlight than small leaves.

Rain Forest

What helps protect plants?

Spines help some plants stay safe.
Spines keep some animals away.

Look at the spines on the thistle plant.

Spines

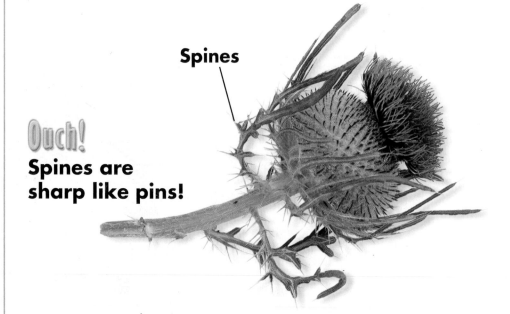

Ouch!
Spines are sharp like pins!

Look at the flowers of the stone plants.
The flowers are hidden in the leaves.

These are stone plants.
Camouflage makes the plants hard to see.
Camouflage keeps the plants safe.
Their roots and stems are in the ground.
What you see are the leaves.

✔ **Lesson Checkpoint**

1. How do spines protect a plant?

2. **Math** in Science   Can you see more thistle plants or more stone plants on these pages?

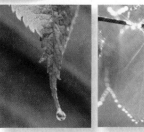

Investigate Which leaf shape drips faster?

Materials

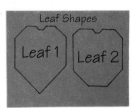

leaf shapes

scissors

tub with water

What to Do

1 Cut out the leaf shapes.

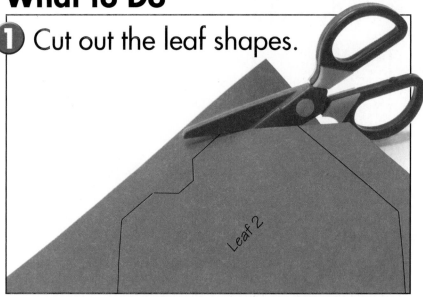

2 Dip the leaf shapes in water.

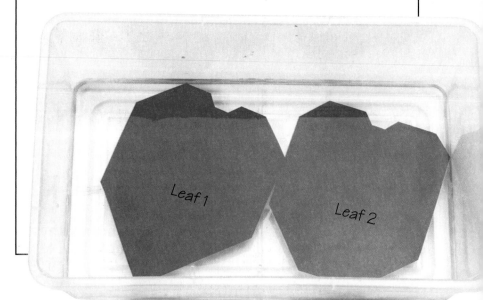

3 Hold up your leaf shapes over the tub.

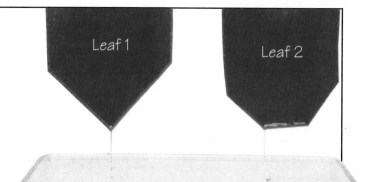

Leaf 1

Leaf 2

4 **Observe** how your leaf shapes drip.

5 Record in the chart.

Leaf Shapes	Fast or Slow Dripping
Leaf 1	
Leaf 2	

Explain Your Results

1. Which leaf shape drips faster?

2. **Infer** Which shape would help a real leaf dry off faster? Why?

Go Further

What would happen if you use 2 real leaves? Try it and find out.

Classify Animals

Look at these animals.
These animals can be sorted
in different ways.

Ways to Sort Animals			
Animal	Fur or Feathers	Wings or No Wings	Teeth or Beak
lion	fur	no wings	sharp teeth
owl	feathers	wings	beak
giraffe	fur	no wings	flat teeth
cardinal	feather	wings	beak
rabbit	fur	no wings	teeth
deer	fur	no wings	teeth
kangaroo	fur	no wings	teeth

Use the chart to answer these questions.

1. What kind of body covering does an owl have?
2. Do more of these animals move with wings or no wings?

Lab zone **Take-Home Activity**

Draw three different animals. Make a chart to classify them by size and by color.

Vocabulary

Which picture goes with each word?

1. antennae
2. camouflage
3. leaf
4. root
5. stem
6. flower

What did you learn?

7. What are three different ways animals move?

8. How do the parts of a plant help it grow?

9. What parts of a plant help protect it from animals?

10. Communicate Tell how the shape of a leaf can help water drip off it.

Alike and Different

11. How are these plants **alike and different**?

Alike	Different

Test Prep

Fill in the circle next to the correct answer.

12. What part of a plant makes seeds?

    Ⓐ stem

    Ⓑ flower

    Ⓒ root

    Ⓓ leaf

13. Writing in Science Write a sentence about how camouflage helps keep living things safe.

Medical Researcher

Read Together

Dr. Todd Schlegel and Dr. Jude DePalma worked at NASA to create a machine that helps doctors see how astronauts' hearts work.

Dr. Schlegel is looking for ways to help astronauts who have medical problems while they are on long trips into space.

Doctors can use the machine to see if astronauts' hearts work the same way on Earth and in space. If doctors see that an astronaut's heart is having problems in space, then they will be able to help the astronaut get better.

Dr. DePalma wants the heart machine to help doctors all over the world too.

Lab zone Take-Home Activity

Draw a picture of how you help people. Share your picture with your family.

80

EC NTL 10 9 8 7 6 5 4

Chapter 4
Life Cycles

You Will Discover

- how animals change as they grow.
- how plants change as they grow.

online
Student Edition
sfsuccessnet.com

How do animals and plants grow and change?

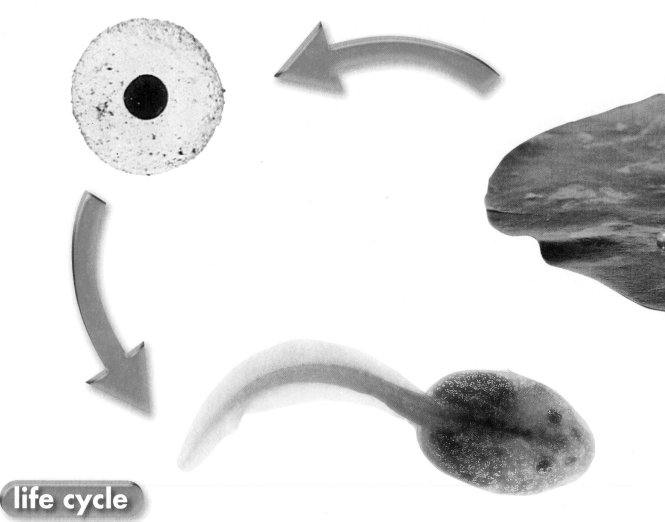

life cycle

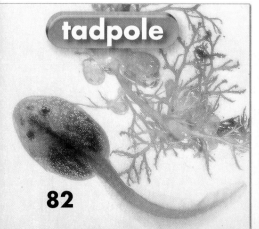

tadpole

larva

82

pupa

seed coat

seedling

83

Explore How do mealworms change as they grow?

Materials

home with mealworms

hand lens

What to Do

1 Use your hand lens. Observe the mealworms every day.

2 Draw and write about the mealworms.

They are alive! Handle with care.

Process Skills

When you **communicate**, you tell what you observe.

Explain Your Results

Communicate Tell how the mealworms change.

Put Things in Order

To put things in order means to tell what happens first, next, and last.

Science Pictures

Apply It!

Look at the pictures. **Communicate** Tell which one comes first, next, and last.

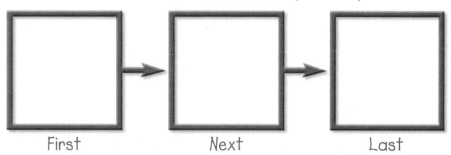

| First | Next | Last |

85

You Are There

That's a Life Cycle

Sung to the tune of "Pop Goes the Weasel"
Lyrics by Gerri Brioso & Richard Freitas/The Dovetail Group, Inc.

Let's play a game of "First, Next, Last"
So all of us will know,
How things change before our eyes
As they grow and grow.

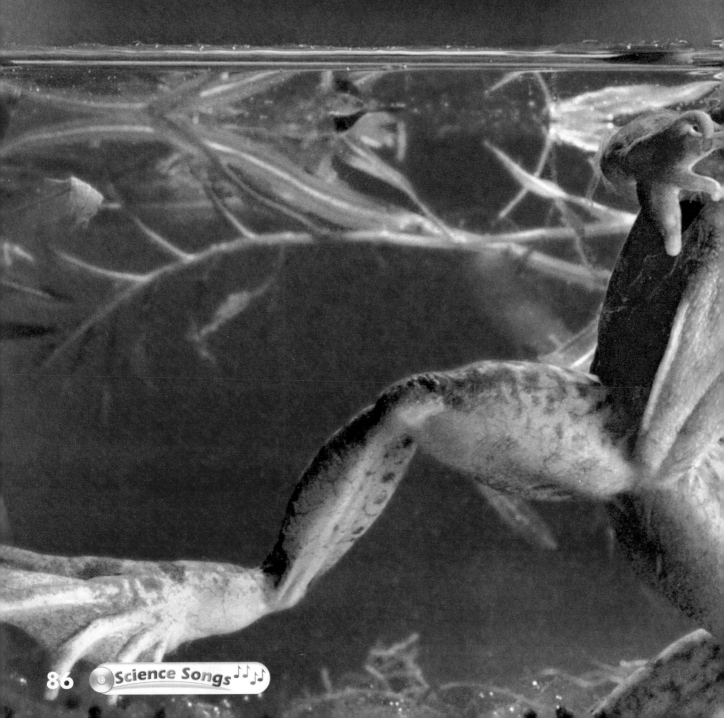

Science Songs

Lesson 1

How does a frog grow?

The frog begins as an egg.
The frog egg hatches.
Out swims a tadpole!
A **tadpole** is a very
young frog.

**A frog egg is tiny.
The egg feels like
jelly.**

**A tadpole has a tail.
A tadpole lives in water.**

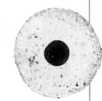

Tadpole

The tadpole swims in water.
The tadpole grows and changes.

This tadpole is five weeks old. Its back legs begin to grow.

Now the tadpole is nine weeks old. Its front legs begin to grow.

The young frog is still growing. Its legs are getting stronger. Soon the young frog will be a grown frog.

This young frog is twelve weeks old. Its tail is getting smaller.

1. ✓Checkpoint How does a tadpole change as it grows?

2. Math in Science Make a time line of the growing frog. Draw when it is an egg and how it looks at 5, 9, and 12 weeks old.

Grown Frog

The tadpole grows into a frog.
The grown frog lives on
land and in water.
The frog hops on land.

Animals grow and change.
All of these changes are
called a **life cycle.**
Look at all the changes
in the frog's life cycle.

First, a frog starts
life as an egg.

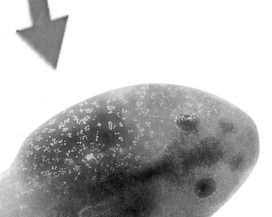

Next, a tadpole
hatches from the
egg. The tadpole
swims in the water.

Last, the tadpole grows into a frog. The grown frog may lay eggs in the water.

☑ Lesson Checkpoint

1. How do frogs and tadpoles move?

2. 🎯 **Put Things in Order**
   Tell about the life cycle of a frog.
   What happens first, next, and last?

How does a butterfly grow?

The butterfly begins as an egg.
A larva hatches from the egg.
A **larva** is a young insect.
The butterfly larva is called
a caterpillar.

First, the butterfly is a tiny egg.

A caterpillar becomes a
pupa when it is changing
inside a hard covering.
Out flies a grown butterfly.

Next, the butterfly becomes a caterpillar. A caterpillar is a butterfly larvae.

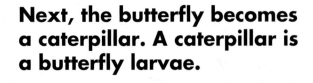

Last, the butterfly has wings to fly. A grown butterfly may lay eggs. The life cycle goes on.

Then, the larva changes into a pupa.

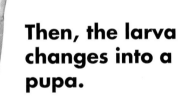

✔ **Lesson Checkpoint**

1. What is a larva?

2. **Math** in Science How many steps are there in the life cycle of a butterfly?

Lesson 3

How do animals grow and change?

Young animals change as they grow.
Young animals change size.
Young animals change shape.

The young salamander lives in water.

Look at how the salamander changes.

The grown salamander lives on land. How are the young salamander and the grown salamander different?

94

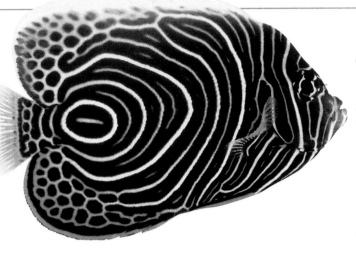

The young angelfish
has spots and swirls.
Its pattern will change.

The grown angelfish has a
pattern of lines. How are
the young angelfish and
the grown angelfish alike
and different?

1. ✓Checkpoint Tell two ways that animals
   may change as they grow.

2. Art in Science Draw and color a young
   angelfish. Draw and color a grown
   angelfish.

Growing Up

Young animals may look like their parents when they grow up. Will young animals look exactly like their parents?

Not always! Young animals may have a different color or pattern. They may be a different size.

Kittens will grow up to be cats.

A grown cat may have a different color pattern than its kittens.

One puppy may grow bigger than the other puppies.

The dogs are different colors. The dogs are different sizes.

✓ **Lesson Checkpoint**

1. How do animals look different from their parents?

2. **Writing** in Science Write two sentences about how these dogs and puppies look **alike and different**.

How does a daisy grow?

Plants have a life cycle.
Most plants grow from seeds.
A **seed coat** covers the seed.
A seed coat protects the seed.

A seedling will grow
from the seed.
A **seedling** is a
very young plant.

First, the life cycle of a daisy begins with a seed.

Next, a seedling begins to grow. The seedling has roots and a stem.

Last, the seedling grows into a plant with flowers. The flowers make seeds. The seeds may grow into new plants.

✓ Lesson Checkpoint

1. How does a seed coat help a seed?

2. **Put Things in Order** What happens first, next, and last in the life cycle of a daisy?

How do trees grow?

A tree grows from a seed.
A tree changes as it grows.
A tree takes many years
to grow.

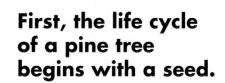

First, the life cycle of a pine tree begins with a seed.

Next, a seedling begins to grow. The seedling has roots and a stem.

Last, the seedling grows into a pine tree. The pine tree makes pinecones. The pinecones make seeds. The seeds may grow into new seedlings.

1. ✓Checkpoint What part of a pine tree makes seeds? How is this different from a daisy?

2. Writing in Science Write in your **science journal,** tell how a seed grows into a pine tree.

How a Cherry Tree Grows

A cherry is a fruit.
A cherry comes from a cherry tree.
The pictures show how
a cherry tree changes.

First, it is spring. The cherry tree has many flowers. The flowers lose their petals. Cherries begin to form.

Last, it is fall. Find the seed inside the cherry. A new cherry tree may grow from the seed.

Next, it is summer. The cherries grow on the tree all summer.

✓ **Lesson Checkpoint**

1. What will grow from the flowers on the cherry trees?

2. **Social Studies** in Science There are many cherry trees in Washington, D.C. Find this city on a map of the United States.

Lesson 6

How do plants grow and change?

Young plants change as they grow.
Look at how the tulip changes.

a tulip beginning to grow

a tulip with a flower

Tulips have different color patterns.

Tulips have different kinds of petals.

The oak seedling has a thin stem.
The oak seedling has
small leaves.
The oak seedling will grow.
It will start to look like the
grown oak tree.

oak seedling

The grown oak tree
has a thick trunk.
The grown oak tree
has big leaves.

grown oak tree

✓ **Lesson Checkpoint**

1. How are the tulips alike
   and different?

2. **Art** in Science Find two leaves from
   the same kind of tree. Put them under
   paper. Rub the paper with a crayon.
   Tell how the leaves are different.

Investigate How do seeds change?

Materials

paper towels

cups

water

bean seeds

radish seeds

daisy seeds

What to Do

1 Fold a paper towel and put it inside a cup.

2 Ball up another paper towel and put it inside the same cup.

3 Wet the paper towels with water.

4 Put the bean seeds in the cup.

5 Repeat the steps with radish seeds. Repeat the steps with daisy seeds.

6 Observe the seeds for 10 days. **Collect Data** Draw what you see.

Seed Changes			
	Bean	**Radish**	**Daisy**
Day 1			
Day 2			
Day 3			

Explain Your Results

1. What changes did you see in the different seeds?

2. **Infer** If you planted radish seeds and bean seeds in your garden, which would grow first?

Go Further

How would the seeds grow in soil? Make a plan to find out.

Comparing Size and Age

As people grow, their size changes.
The girl in this picture has grown.

The table shows how tall the girl was when she was two, six, and ten years old.

Age	Size
2 years old	2 feet tall
6 years old	4 feet tall
10 years old	5 feet tall

1. How old was the girl when she was two feet tall?
2. How many feet did the girl grow from when she was six years old to when she was ten years old?

Lab zone Take-Home Activity

Make a table. Show the age of each person in your family. Write the names of the people in order from youngest to oldest.

Vocabulary

Which picture goes with each word?

1. tadpole

2. larva

3. pupa

4. seedling

5. seed coat

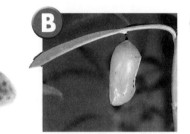

What did you learn?

6. How is a larva different from a butterfly?

7. What is one way to guess what a young animal will look like when it is grown?

8. Plants and animals grow and change. What are all of these changes called?

9. Collect Data Find out how many people in your class have pets.

Put Things in Order

10. Look at the pictures. Tell which one comes first, next, and last.

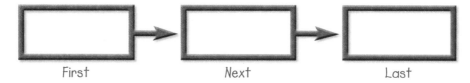

First   Next   Last

Test Prep

Fill in the circle next to the correct answer.

11. What is inside a pinecone?

Ⓐ a daisy

Ⓑ seeds

Ⓒ needles

Ⓓ a tree

12. **Writing** in Science Write a poem about how the cherry tree changes during the year.

Doctors

Read Together

Doctors help people stay healthy. People go to a doctor for a checkup. Doctors check people as they grow and change.

Doctors work to keep everyone in a family healthy.

The doctor will look at a person's eyes and ears. The doctor will listen to a person's heart. The doctor will ask people questions about how they feel. The doctor will answer questions too.

Doctors try to help sick people get well. The doctor might give a sick person medicine. Some medicines help a person feel better.

Lab zone Take-Home Activity

Make a poster. Tell some of the things that doctors do to help people stay healthy.

You Will Discover

- that some plants make their own food.
- what animals eat for food.

Chapter 5

Food Chains

How are living things connected?

food chain

oxygen

Oxygen is a gas in the air that plants and animals need to live.

rain forest

114

marsh

Round and Round and Round

Sung to the tune of "The Wheels on the Bus"
Lyrics by Gerri Brioso & Richard Freitas/The Dovetail Group, Inc.

The plant uses sunlight
to make its food.

Make its food.

Make its food.

The plant uses Sun to make its food.

To grow and grow and grow.

How do plants and animals get food?

All living things need food.
Even you!

What do animals eat?
Some animals eat plants.
Some animals eat other animals.
Some animals eat plants
and animals.

Plants Make Food

Plants need food.
Leaves of green plants make food.
You might wonder how.

Roots take in water from soil.
The water goes up the stem
to the leaves.

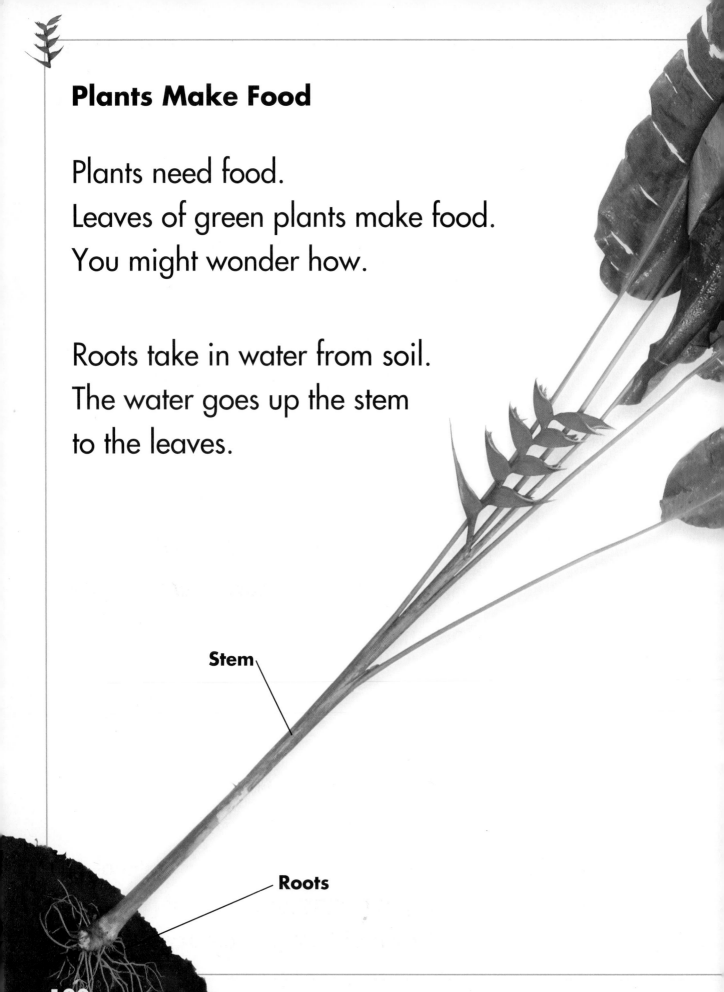

Stem

Roots

Leaves

Green leaves take in sunlight.
Green leaves take in air.
Green leaves use sunlight,
air, and water to make food.

Green leaves give off oxygen
when they make food.
Oxygen is a gas in the air.
Plants and animals need
oxygen to live.

✔️ **Lesson Checkpoint**

1. Why are green leaves important
   to plants?

2. 🎯 **Draw Conclusions** What
   might happen to animals if plant
   leaves did not give off oxygen?

How do living things get food in a rain forest?

A **rain forest** is a habitat.
A rain forest gets lots of rain.

The plant below grows in a rain forest.
The plant uses sunlight to make food.

The katydid eats the plant for food.
The lizard eats the katydid for food.

Crunch!
**The katydid
bites the plant.**

Zap!
**The small lizard will
catch the katydid.**

Swoop!

The bird will catch the small lizard.

The bird sees the lizard. The hungry bird eats the lizard for food.

1. ✓Checkpoint What does the katydid eat for food?

2. 🎯 **Draw Conclusions** What might happen to the bird if there were no lizards to eat?

Food for Animals

The hungry tayra spots the bird.
The tayra will catch the bird.
The tayra will eat the bird for food.

Pounce!

The tayra will leap at the bird.

124

The plant makes food.
The katydid eats the plant.
The lizard eats the katydid.
The bird eats the lizard.
The tayra eats the bird.

This is called a **food chain.**
All living things are connected
through food chains.

Tayra

Bird

Lizard

Katydid

**Plant takes
in sunlight**

✓**Lesson Checkpoint**

1. What does the tayra eat for food?

2. **Writing** in Science Write a sentence
about the food chain in a rain forest.

How do living things get food in a marsh?

There are food chains in a marsh.
A **marsh** is a wetland habitat.

The marsh plant uses sunlight to make food. The rat will eat the plant for food.

The hungry snake slithers toward the rat.
The snake will eat the rat for food.

Gulp!
**The snake will
catch the rat.**

1. ✓Checkpoint How are the
plant and the rat connected?

2. Writing in Science Write a
sentence about an animal in the
marsh. Tell how it gets food.

Finding Food

The bird is hungry.
The bird sees the snake.
The bird will fly down
and catch the snake.
The bird will eat the snake.

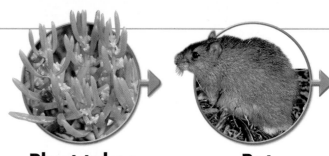

Plant takes in sunlight

Rat

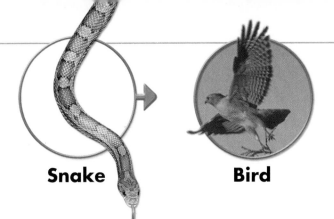

Snake   **Bird**

The plant uses sunlight
to make food.
The rat eats the plant.
The snake eats the rat.
The bird eats the snake.
This is one kind of food chain
in a marsh.

Nibble, nibble!
The bird will eat
the snake for food.

☑ **Lesson Checkpoint**

1. How do animals in a marsh
   get food?

2. **Math** in Science Put the marsh
   food chain in order. Use words
   such as *first* and *second*.

Investigate How can you make a model of a food chain?

Materials

crayons or markers

paper plates

tape

yarn

Process Skills

You use what you learn to **make a definition** of a food chain.

What to Do

1 Draw the plant. Show the sun in your drawing.

2 Draw the rat, snake, and bird from the marsh.

3 **Make a model** of a food chain. Connect your drawings with tape and yarn.

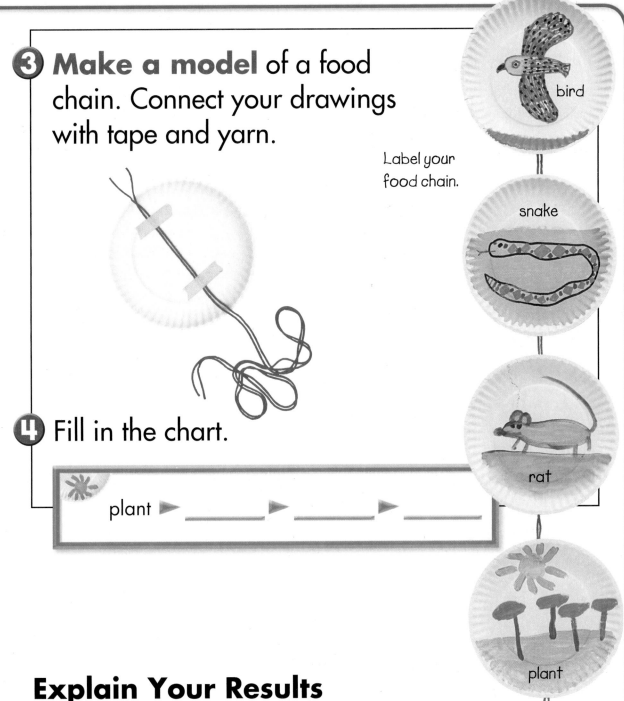

Label your food chain.

bird

snake

rat

plant

4 Fill in the chart.

plant ▶ _____ ▶ _____ ▶ _____

Explain Your Results

1. Tell about your model. **Make a definition** of a food chain.

2. How is your model like a real food chain in a marsh?

Go Further

What is another way to model a food chain? Make a model to show your idea.

Grouping Animals

Look at the Venn diagram.
It groups animals by what they eat.

Grouping Animals by What They Eat

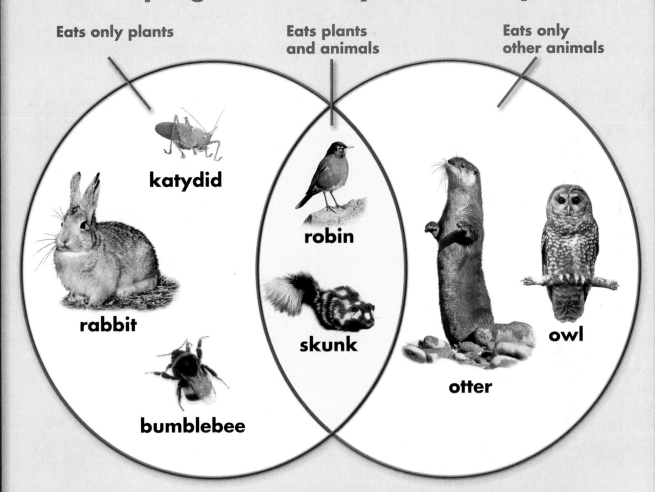

Eats only plants

Eats plants
and animals

Eats only
other animals

katydid

rabbit

bumblebee

robin

skunk

otter

owl

Use the Venn diagram to answer the questions.
1. How many of these animals eat only plants?
2. How many animals eat both plants and
   animals?
3. How many animals eat only other animals?

Lab zone Take-Home Activity

Find pictures of animals.
Work with someone in your
family to sort the animals.
Make a Venn diagram that
shows what the animals eat.

Vocabulary

Which picture goes with each word?

1. food chain
2. rain forest
3. marsh

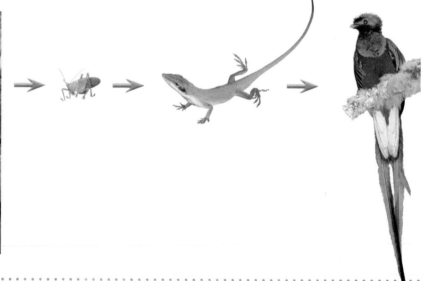

What did you learn?

4. What is oxygen?
5. What do animals eat?
6. How are all living things connected?

7. Make a definition of a marsh using what you learned in this chapter.

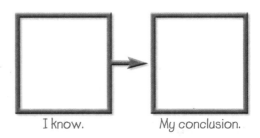

I know. → My conclusion.

Draw Conclusions

8. What do you think the bear will eat? **Draw conclusions.**

The bear is looking for food.

Test Prep

Fill in the circle next to the correct answer.

9. What is one kind of wetland habitat?

Ⓐ meadow

Ⓑ desert

Ⓒ marsh

Ⓓ forest

10. Writing in Science What do leaves use to make food? Make a list.

Entomologists

Read Together

Insects are animals that live all over the world. Entomologists learn how insects help plants and animals. Entomologists learn how insects harm plants and animals.

Entomologists learn which insects eat plants. Entomologists learn which plants and animals eat insects.

Insects have three body parts. Insects have six legs.

Entomologists learn about insects in their habitats.

Lab zone Take-Home Activity

What insect would you like to observe? Tell your family.

Unit A Test Talk

Test-Taking Strategies

▶ Find Important Words
Choose the Right Answer
Use Information from Text and Graphics
Write Your Answer

Find Important Words

Read the story.

Squirrel

Mark saw a squirrel in his yard.
The squirrel was eating seeds.
The squirrel was hiding seeds too.

Read the question.

What was the squirrel eating?

Ⓐ leaves

Ⓑ seeds

Ⓒ yard

Ⓓ hiding

Find important words in the question.
Find important words in the story that match
the words in the question. Answer the question.

Unit A Wrap-Up

Chapter 1

What do living things need?
- Plants need air, water, sunlight, and space to live.
- Animals need food, water, and shelter.

Chapter 2

Where do plants and animals live?
- Plants and animals live in different habitats.

Chapter 3

How do parts help living things?
- Different parts help animals get food and live in their habitats.
- Different parts help plants get water and make food in their habitats.

Chapter 4

How do animals and plants grow and change?
- Animals and plants grow and change in different ways. These changes are called a life cycle.

Chapter 5

How are living things connected?
- Living things are connected through food chains.

Performance Assessment

Make a Model Using Camouflage

- Make a model of an animal.
- Use camouflage on your model.
- Hide your model in your classroom.
- Tell how the camouflage made the model hard to see.

Read More About Life Science!

Look for books like these in your library.

Experiment How can camouflage help mice stay hidden from hawks?

Model camouflage. White beans are the field where mice live. Black beans are black mice. Beans with spots are white mice.

Materials

3 bags of beans

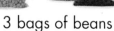

paper plate

timer

Ask a question.
How can camouflage help some mice stay hidden from hawks?

Make a hypothesis.
Are white beans with spots or black beans easier to see on a white background?

Plan a fair test.
Use the same number of black beans and white beans with spots.

Do your test.

1 One person is the hawk. The hawk must turn away.

2 Put the white beans on the plate. Add 10 black beans and 10 white beans with spots. Mix the beans.

3 Let the hawk turn around and pick up mice with one hand.

4 Take turns being the hawk. Record how many beans you pick up.

Listen for "Go" and "Stop."

Mice   Field

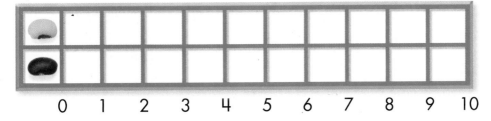

Collect and record data.

Number of beans

0   1   2   3   4   5   6   7   8   9   10

Tell your conclusion.
Which beans were harder to see? Which mice are harder to see in a white habitat?

Go Further
What if you added red beans? Experiment to find out.

The Frog on the Log

by Ilo Orleans

There once
Was a green
    Little frog, frog, frog—

Who played
In the wood
    On a log, log, log!

A screech owl
Sitting
    In a tree, tree, tree—

Came after
The frog
  With a scree, scree, scree!

When the frog
Heard the owl—
  In a flash, flash, flash—

He leaped
In the pond
  With a splash, splash, splash!

143

Science Fair Projects

Full Inquiry

Using Scientific Methods

1. Ask a question.
2. Make a hypothesis.
3. Plan a fair test.
4. Do your test.
5. Collect and record data.
6. Tell your conclusion.
7. Go further.

Idea 1

Growing Plants in Soil

Plan a project.
Find out which kind
of soil is best for plants.

Idea 2

What Birds Eat

Plan a project.
Find out which
kinds of foods
birds like.

EC NTL 10 9 8 7 6 5 4

Unit B

Earth Science

You Will Discover
- what makes up Earth.
- how people can help protect Earth.

Chapter 6
Land, Water, and Air

online
Student Edition
sfsuccessnet.com

How are land, water, and air important?

sand

clay

humus

rocks

weathering

natural resource

erosion

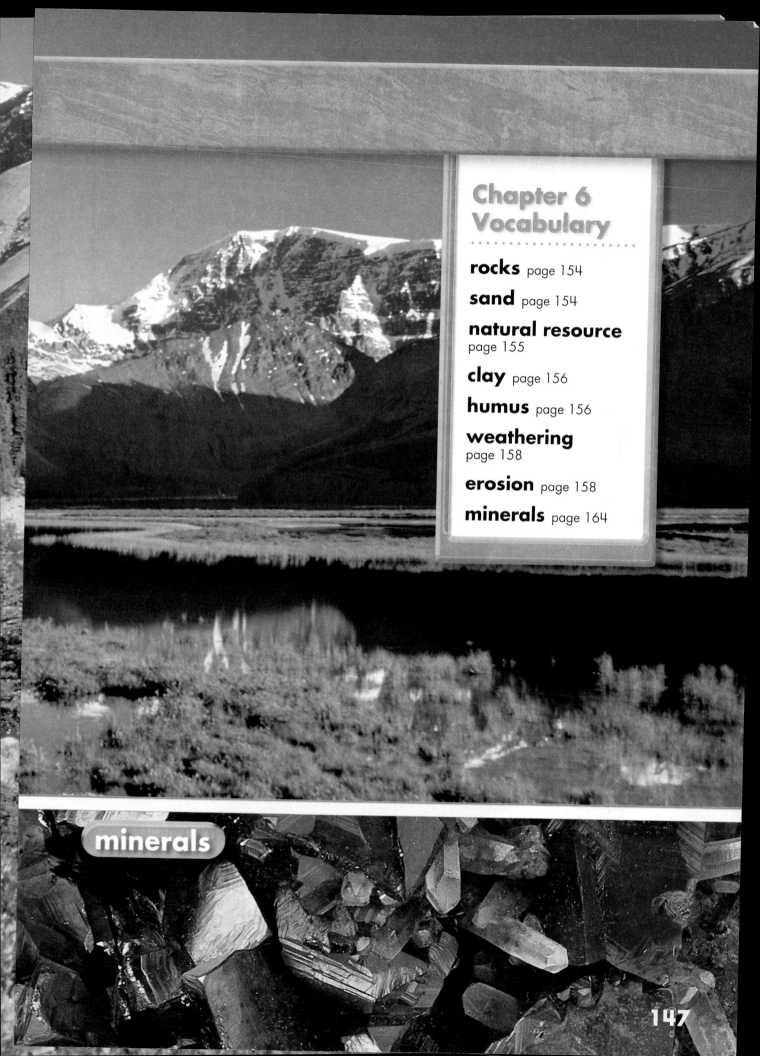

Chapter 6 Vocabulary

minerals

147

Water, Air, and Land

Sung to the tune of "I've Been Working On the Railroad"
Lyrics by Gerri Brioso & Richard Freitas/The Dovetail Group, Inc.

Earth is made of land and water.

Air is all around.

Earth is made of land and water.

And look what else I found.

What makes up Earth?

Look at the picture.
Find the land.
Find the water.
Land and water make up the surface
of Earth.
There is more water than land on Earth.

Kinds of Land and Water

Different kinds of land and water are found on Earth.

A plain is flat land.
A hill is where the land gets higher.

hill

plain

This is a lake.
A lake is water that has land all around it.

lake

This is a river.
A river is water that flows through the land.

river

A cliff is land that is very steep.
Look at this cliff.
This cliff is next to the ocean.

✓ **Lesson Checkpoint**

1. What makes up the surface of Earth?

2. 🎯 What is one **important detail** that you saw and read about a lake?

Lesson 2

What are rocks and soil?

Rocks are nonliving things.
Rocks come from Earth.

Rocks can be many colors.
Some rocks feel smooth.
Some rocks feel rough.

Rocks are all different sizes and shapes.
Sand is tiny pieces of broken rock.
Big rocks are called boulders.

Sand   **Small rocks**

SciLinks   Take It to the Net   keyword: rock
sfsuccessnet.com   code: g1p154

The road is made of rocks.

The fox is hiding in the rocks.

Rocks are a natural resource. A **natural resource** is a useful thing that comes from nature.

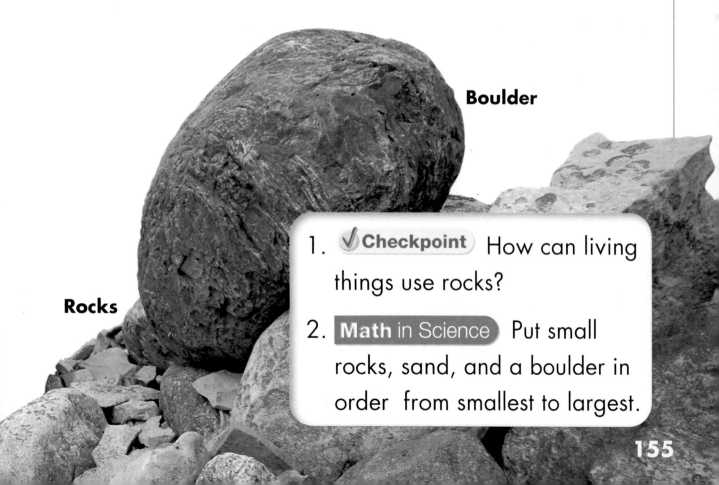

Boulder

Rocks

1. ✓Checkpoint How can living things use rocks?

2. Math in Science Put small rocks, sand, and a boulder in order from smallest to largest.

Soil

Soil is a natural resource.
Soil may have sand, clay, and humus in it.

Sand

Sand feels rough.
Sand is loose and easy to dig.

Clay

Clay is sticky and soft.
It is hard for plants to grow in clay.

Humus

Humus is made of parts of living things that died.

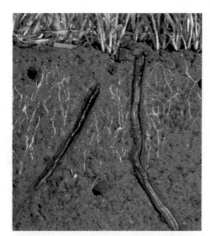

Worms loosen the soil. The loose soil helps plants grow.

Humus in the soil helps plants grow.

1. What helps plants grow?

2.  **Math** in Science How many rabbits are in the picture?

Look at this picture. What lives and grows in the soil?

What changes land?

Weathering can change land.
Weathering happens when
rocks break apart and change.
Water and ice can cause weathering.
Weathering can take a long time!

Erosion can change land.
Erosion happens when wind
or water moves rocks and soil.

Roots of plants
help hold the
soil in place.
Plants can slow
down erosion.

✓ **Lesson Checkpoint**

1. What can change rocks?

2. 🎯 What is one **important**
detail you saw and read
about erosion?

Weathering helped change the shape, size, and color of this rock.

Crack!

Tree roots break the sidewalk as they grow. This is weathering.

Erosion is happening here. The water is washing the soil away quickly.

How can people and animals change the soil?

159

How do living things use natural resources?

Air is a natural resource.
Plants and trees need clean air to grow.
People and animals breathe air.
Some animals fly in the air.

Cars and trucks can give off harmful
materials into the air.
People can help keep the air clean.
People can walk.
People can ride bikes.

Wind is moving air. Look at how the wind blows the leaves of the trees.

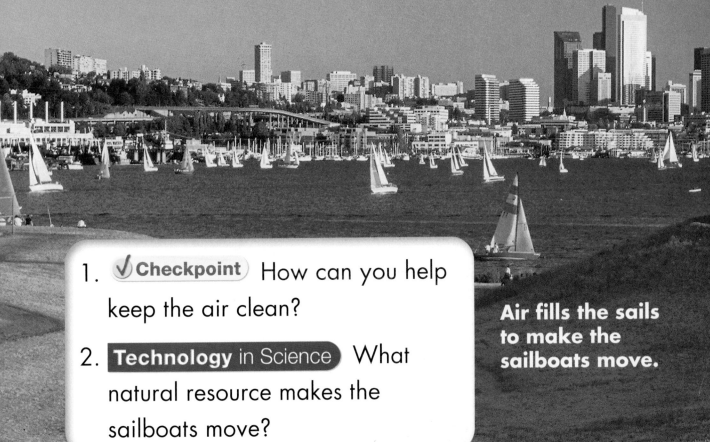

Air fills the sails to make the sailboats move.

1. ✓Checkpoint How can you help keep the air clean?

2. Technology in Science What natural resource makes the sailboats move?

161

Using Water

Water is a natural resource.
Many animals live in water.
Most animals drink water.

Splish!

This crab lives in the ocean. Some people use crabs for food.

People use water for drinking. People use water for bathing and cooking food. What other ways do people use water?

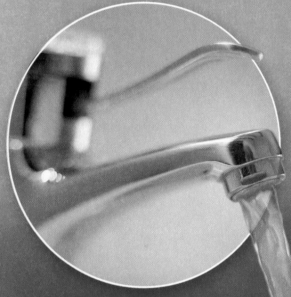

You can save water by turning the water off when brushing your teeth.

Splash!

People swim and play in water.

1. ✓ **Checkpoint** How do animals use water?

2. **Writing** in Science Write in your **science journal.** List three ways that you use water.

Using Land

Land is an important natural resource. The pictures show ways that people use land.

People grow food in soil. People use wood from trees to build things.

Minerals come from the land. **Minerals** are nonliving things. Minerals are found in rocks and soil. Gold, silver, and copper are minerals. People use minerals in different ways.

☑ **Lesson Checkpoint**

1. What is one way that people use land?

2. **Writing** in Science Write a sentence that describes minerals.

Carrots grow in soil. What other foods that you eat grow in soil?

Trees grow on land. Name some things made from wood.

minerals

pennies

People use copper to make pennies.

You can help keep the land clean. You can put trash in a trash can.

How can you reduce, reuse, and recycle?

You can help save Earth's land, water, and air.
You can reduce, reuse, and recycle.

Reduce means to use less.

Reuse means to use things again.

Recycle means to make old things into new things.

You can carry food in a cloth bag. This will help reduce the paper you use.

You can reuse an old jug. It can be a pot for plants.

Old papers can be recycled to make boxes.

Glass bottles can be recycled to make glass beads.

✓ **Lesson Checkpoint**

1. What are three ways to help save Earth's resources?

2. **Art** in Science Make a poster. Show others how to reduce, reuse, and recycle.

Investigate How are these soils different?

Materials

cups with soils

hand lens

cup with water

dropper

3 craft sticks

What to Do

① **Observe** the soils.

② **Collect Data** Draw and write about the dry soils. Use the word bank.

③ Add water and stir.

Process Skills

Recording in a chart is a way to **collect data** about soils.

④ Draw and write about the wet soils.
Use the word bank.

clay

Word Bank

sticky	red
crumbly	brown
dusty	black
sandy	

	Dry	Wet
Humus		
Sand		
Clay		

Explain Your Results

1. **Communicate** How did the soils change when you added water?

2. Which of the soils have you seen? Tell where.

Go Further

What is the soil like where you live? Investigate to find out.

Math in Science

Reading a Picture Graph

Look at the picture graph. It shows what the children at West School found in their school's recycling bin.

eTools Take It to the Net
sfsuccessnet.com

Use the picture graph to answer the questions.

What children found in their recycling bin.					
Juice Boxes	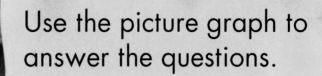				
Cans					
Paper					
Plastic Bottles					

1. Are there more cans or bottles in the recycling bin?
2. How many things are there to recycle in all?

Lab zone Take-Home Activity

Collect cans used by your family. Collect boxes used by your family. Make a picture graph. Show how many cans and boxes your family can recycle.

Vocabulary

Which picture goes with each word?

1. rocks
2. sand
3. clay
4. humus
5. erosion
6. minerals

A

B

C

D

E

F

What did you learn?

7. What is weathering?

8. Why is land an important natural resource?

9. How do you use water and air?

10. Collect Data Name things in your classroom that can be recycled or reused.

Important Details

11. What are two **important details** you saw and read about Lily's shoebox?

Lily's Shoebox

Lily is using a shoebox. She is using it to hold her CDs.

Lily's shoebox

Test Prep

Fill in the circle that correctly answers the question.

12. What makes up the surface of Earth?
Ⓐ sun and moon
Ⓑ water and land
Ⓒ plants and animals
Ⓓ summer and winter

13. Writing in Science Write two sentences. Tell how people can protect the land.

Satellites Help Scientists Find Fossils

NASA Landsat satellites go around Earth. Landsat satellites send information about land on Earth. This information helps some scientists find places to look for fossils.

A fossil is a part or a print of a plant or animal that lived long ago. Some fossils are found in rocks. Look at the pictures of fossils on the next page.

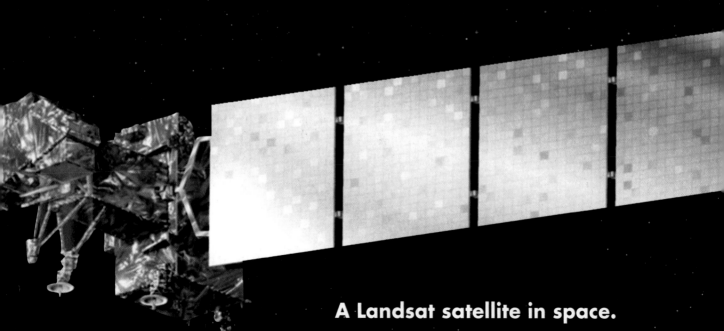

A Landsat satellite in space.

Fossils can teach us about animals that lived on Earth. Fossils can teach us about Earth's past.

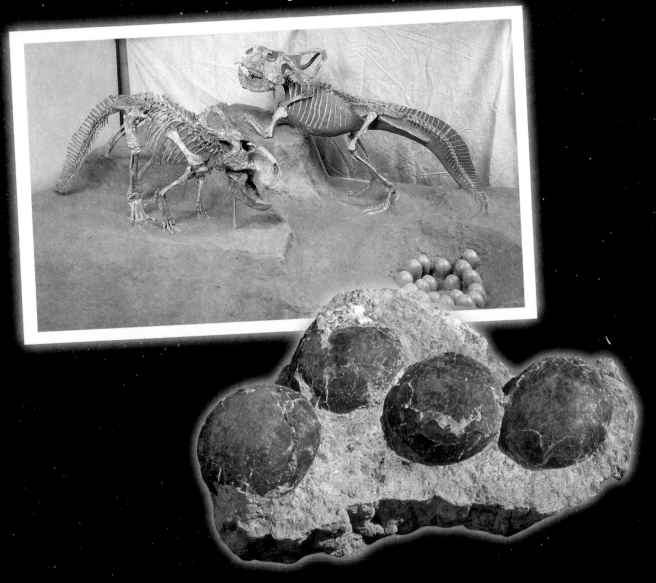

This is a fossil of dinosaur eggs.

Lab zone **Take-Home Activity**

Find a tree leaf. Draw what you think the fossil of the tree leaf will look like.

Geologist and Paleontologist
Dr. Winifred Goldring

Read Together

Winifred Goldring loved rocks and fossils when she was young. She became a geologist and a paleontologist when she grew up. A geologist studies rocks. A paleontologist studies fossils.

First, Dr. Goldring was a teacher. Then, she set up rocks and fossils for people to look at in a museum. Dr. Goldring also wrote books about rocks and fossils.

Dr. Goldring studied this National Historic Landmark called the "Grotto."

Dr. Goldring was the first female State Paleontologist of New York.

Lab zone Take-Home Activity

Collect some rocks around your neighborhood. Set up your rocks for others to see. Show your rocks to your family.

Chapter 7
Weather

You Will Discover

- what tools are used to measure weather.
- about the seasons.

Web Games
Take It to the Net
sfsuccessnet.com

Discovery Channel School
Student DVD
DISCOVERY CHANNEL SCHOOL

online
Student Edition
sfsuccessnet.com

Weather Tools

You can use a thermometer to see what the weather is like.

A **thermometer** is a tool used to measure temperature. **Temperature** is how hot or cold something is.

All thermometers have numbers. The numbers show temperature.

Whew! It is hot today. The temperature goes up as the air gets warmer.

Brr! It is cold today. The temperature goes down as the air gets cooler.

Sometimes the weather is windy.
People use a tool called a wind vane.
Wind vanes tell the direction of the wind.
A wind vane points into the wind.

Sometimes the weather is rainy.
People use a rain gauge to measure
how much rain falls.

✓ **Lesson Checkpoint**

1. What tool might you use to measure
   air temperature?

2. **Technology** in Science What tools might
   people use in different kinds of weather?

Whoosh!
**The wind is
blowing hard.**

Pitter-patter
Rain is pouring down.

How do clouds form?

There is water in the air.
Water vapor is a form of water
in the air. You cannot see water vapor.

Clouds form when water vapor cools.
Clouds are made of tiny drops of water or
pieces of ice.

Clouds have many shapes and sizes.
Different clouds bring different kinds
of weather.

√ Lesson Checkpoint

1. What makes up clouds?

2. Observe the clouds in the sky.
   Predict the weather.

These clouds are very high in the sky. These clouds are signs of good weather.

These fluffy clouds are signs of good weather too.

These dark gray clouds are signs of storms.

Fog is made of tiny water drops. Fog is a cloud that is near the ground. It is hard to see in fog.

187

What are some kinds of wet weather?

Rain is one kind of wet weather. Many animals look for shelter when it rains. The animals want to stay dry. Many people look for shelter too. How can you stay dry in the rain?

Plants need rain.
Plants get water from rain.
Plants need water to live.

This snake finds shelter from the rain.

These children are keeping dry in the rain.

A plant needs rain to grow.

It is cold outside.
Rain may change into sleet.
Sleet is frozen rain.
Sleet is another kind of wet weather.

1. ✅ **Checkpoint** What are two kinds of wet weather?

2. **Math** in Science Make a chart. Show how many days this week had sun, clouds, or rain.

Snowy Weather

The temperature went down.
Snow began to fall.

Snow is water that freezes high in the air.
Snow falls in very cold weather.
Snow is a kind of wet weather.

These bears live where
there is a lot of snow.
These bears have thick fur.
Thick fur helps the bears
stay warm.

Look at how much snow fell during this blizzard.

A blizzard is a snowstorm.
A lot of snow falls during a blizzard.
Strong winds blow the snow.

✓ Lesson Checkpoint

1. What is a blizzard?

2. **Predict** Tell what clothes you might wear if it started to snow.

Lesson 4

What are the four seasons?

A **season** is a time of year.
The four seasons are spring,
summer, fall, and winter.
Spring comes after winter.

spring

It is warm in
the spring.

summer

Summer comes after
spring. Summer is
warmer than spring.

The pattern of the seasons begins again.
What are the seasons like where you live?

✓ **Lesson Checkpoint**

1. Tell the four seasons in order. Begin with spring.

2. **Writing** in Science Write in your **science journal.** Tell about winter where you live.

Fall comes after summer. Fall is cooler than summer.

Winter comes after fall. Winter is the coldest season of the year.

Investigate How does the temperature change each day?

Materials

thermometer

red crayons

What to Do

1 **Measure** the temperature outside for 5 days. Measure the temperature at the same time each day.

2 **Collect Data** Show the temperature each day. Use a red crayon.

3 Compare the temperatures.

Temperature				
Day 1	**Day 2**	**Day 3**	**Day 4**	**Day 5**

Explain Your Results

1. How can you tell which day you recorded the warmest temperatures?

2. **Interpret Data** Which day did you measure the coldest temperature?

Go Further
How does the temperature change from month to month where you live? Make a plan to find out.

Using a Bar Graph

Map Facts

Cincinnati, Ohio, usually gets about 121 cm of rain each year.

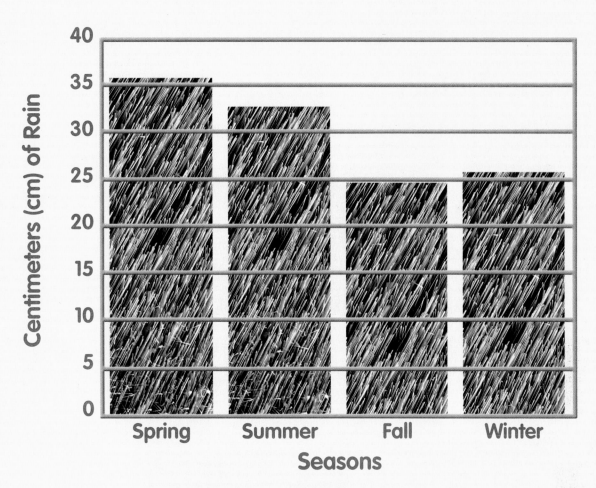

Rainfall in Cincinnati, Ohio

Use the bar graph to answer these questions.
1. Which season gets the most rain in Cincinnati, Ohio?
2. Which season gets the least rain in Cincinnati, Ohio?

Lab zone Take-Home Activity

Use a rain gauge to measure how much rain falls where you live each day. Make a bar graph to show how much rain falls each day in a week.

Vocabulary

Which picture goes with each word?

1. cloud

2. sleet

3. thermometer

What did you learn?

4. What is weather?

5. What tools are used to measure weather?

6. What is water vapor?

7. What is the warmest season of the year?

8. Predict The sky is full of dark gray clouds. Predict what the weather might be like.

Predict

9. Suppose the summer is very dry. **Predict** what might happen to this plant.

I know.   I predict.

Test Prep

Fill in the circle next to the correct answer.

10. What is used to measure temperature?

  Ⓐ rain gauge

  Ⓑ season

  Ⓒ thermometer

  Ⓓ wind vane

11. Writing in Science   Write how some animals might stay warm in snowy weather.

Meteorologist

Dr. J. Marshall Shepherd is a research meteorologist at NASA.

Read Together

A meteorologist is a scientist who studies or predicts the weather. First, some meteorologists use special weather tools to collect data.

Next, some meteorologists make special maps about the weather.

Last, some meteorologists share their predictions about what the weather will be like.

Dr. Shepherd does science experiments that help us to better understand Earth and its weather.

Lab zone Take-Home Activity

Look at a weather map in a newspaper. Collect data from the map. Predict what the weather might be like tomorrow.

Unit B Test Talk

Use Information from Text and Graphics

Read the chart and text.

Temperature

Day	Temperature
Monday	10 degrees Celsius
Tuesday	20 degrees Celsius
Wednesday	25 degrees Celsius
Thursday	15 degrees Celsius
Friday	10 degrees Celsius

Juan made a chart of the temperature for five days. Wednesday was the warmest day.

Use the information in the chart and in the text to answer the question.

What was the temperature on the warmest day of the week?

Ⓐ 10 degrees Celsius

Ⓑ 15 degrees Celsius

Ⓒ 25 degrees Celsius

Ⓓ 20 degrees Celsius

The text tells what day was the warmest. Look at the chart to see what the temperature was on that day.

201

Unit B Wrap-Up

Chapter 6

How are land, water, and air important?

- Land and water make up the surface of Earth.
- Land, water, and air are important natural resources.

Chapter 7

What are the four seasons?

- The four seasons are spring, summer, fall, and winter.

Performance Assessment

Make a Poster

- Find pictures in a magazine of people using water.

- Cut the pictures out.

- Make a poster using your pictures. Tell about all the ways that you can use water.

Read More About Earth Science!

Look for books like these in your library.

Lab zone Full Inquiry

Experiment Does the Sun warm land or water faster?

The sunlight warms Earth's land and water during the day. Does the sunlight warm land and water in the same way?

Materials

cup with water and cup with soil

2 thermometers

lamp

Ask a question.
Does sunlight warm the land or water faster?

Make a hypothesis.
Will a cup of soil warm faster than a cup of water? Tell what you think.

Plan a fair test.
Make sure the lamp is placed evenly above both cups.

Do your test.

Process Skills

You **plan a fair test** in an experiment when you choose the one thing that you will change.

1 Put one thermometer in the soil. Put the other thermometer in the water.

The soil is like land.

2 Wait for 30 minutes.
Record the temperatures.

3 Place the lamp so the light shines on both cups.

4 Wait 1 hour.
Record the temperatures.

5 Turn the light off.

The lamp is like the Sun.

Collect and record data.

	Temperature at start	Temperature after 1 hour
Soil		
Water		

Tell your conclusion.

Did soil or water warm faster?
Do you think the Sun warms
land or water faster? Why do
you think so?

Go Further

What if the cups
were under the
lamp for 2 hours?
Try it and find out.

Wind

by Ivy O. Eastwick

Nobody knows
where the Wind goes—
it comes with a flutter
it goes with a gust,
it comes when it will
and it goes where it must
but—
where it goes,
nobody knows.

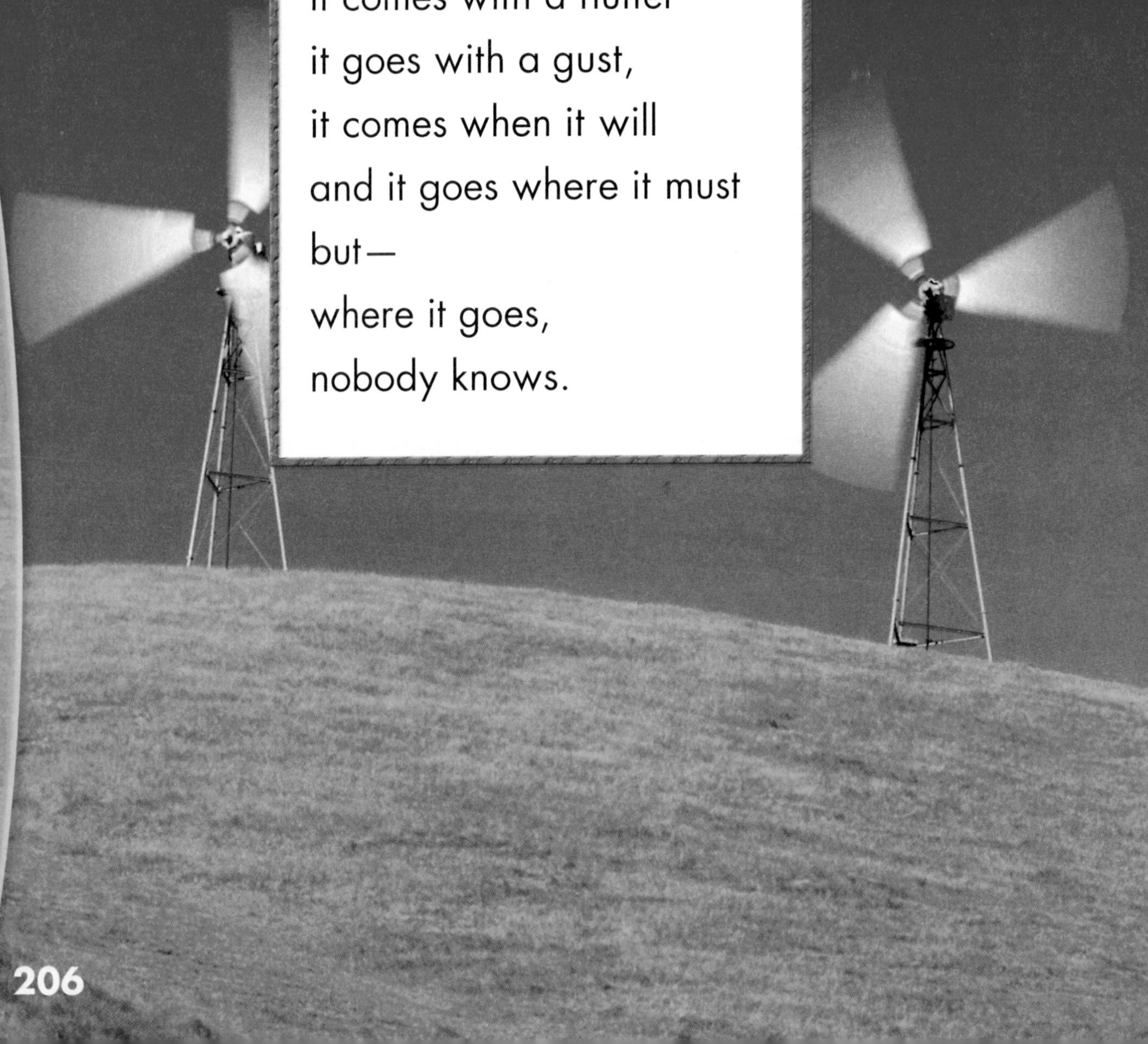

Science Fair Projects

Full Inquiry

Using Scientific Methods
1. Ask a question.
2. Make a hypothesis.
3. Plan a fair test.
4. Do your test.
5. Collect and record data.
6. Tell your conclusion.
7. Go further.

Idea 1
Comparing Temperature

Plan a project. Find out how close predicted temperatures are to actual temperatures.

Idea 2
Erosion

Plan a project. Find out how long it takes erosion to happen in sand, soil, and clay.

Sand   **Clay**   **Soil**

EC NTL 10 9 8 7 6 5 4

Unit C

Physical Science

Chapter 8
Observing Matter

You Will Discover

- ways that matter can be grouped.
- ways that matter can change.

How can objects be described?

liquid

matter

gas

mass

210

solid

dissolve

evaporate

Evaporate means to change from a liquid to a gas.

211

Explore What is in the bags?

Materials

1 2 3 4 5

5 bags with classroom objects

What to Do

1 Take turns reaching into each bag. Touch, smell, and listen.

2 Predict what is in each bag.

3 Look in the bags. Did you predict correctly?

Process Skills

You can **communicate** how touching, smelling, and listening help you predict what is in the bags.

Explain Your Results

Communicate How does touching help you predict?

How to Read Science

 TARGET SKILL

Alike and Different

Alike means how things are the same. Different means how things are not the same.

Science Story

Lemons and Lemonade

Look at the lemon and the cup of lemonade. The lemon is yellow and tastes sour. The lemon has a bumpy coating. The lemonade is yellow and tastes sweet. The lemonade can spill all over the table.

Apply It!
Communicate Tell how the lemon and the lemonade are alike and different.

Alike	Different

♪♫ A "Matter" of Lemonade

Sung to the tune of "Turkey in the Straw"
Lyrics by Gerri Brioso & Richard Freitas/The Dovetail Group, Inc.

When you're making lemonade
you use lemons and cups,
And a great big pitcher that
you will fill up.
Each one has it's own shape
and it takes up space.
All are solid kinds of matter
you can find anyplace.

Science Songs ♪♫

Lesson 1

What is matter?

The pitcher is made of matter.
The drink is made of matter.

Matter is anything that takes
up space.
Matter has many tiny parts.
Matter has mass.

Mass is the amount of matter
in an object.
Everything made of matter has mass.

The lemon is made of matter. Some parts of matter are too small to see without a hand lens.

Describing Matter

The things in the picture
are made of matter.
What shapes do you see?
What colors do you see?
How are the things
alike and different?

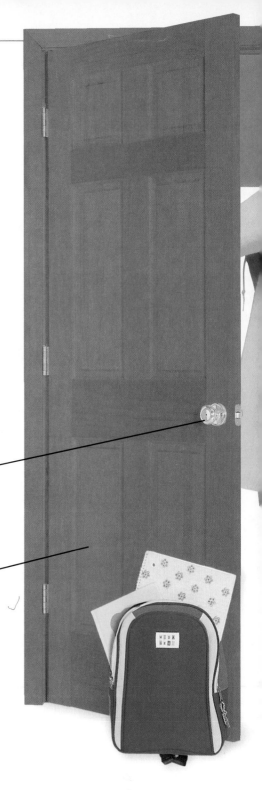

**The door handle
is made of metal.**

**The wood door is a rectangle.
The door feels hard.**

☑ **Lesson Checkpoint**

1. What are two ways you can group
   the things in the picture?

2. **Writing** in Science

   Make a chart like this one.
   Fill it in with words that
   tell about each thing.

	Color	Feel
door		
scarf		
basket		
boots		

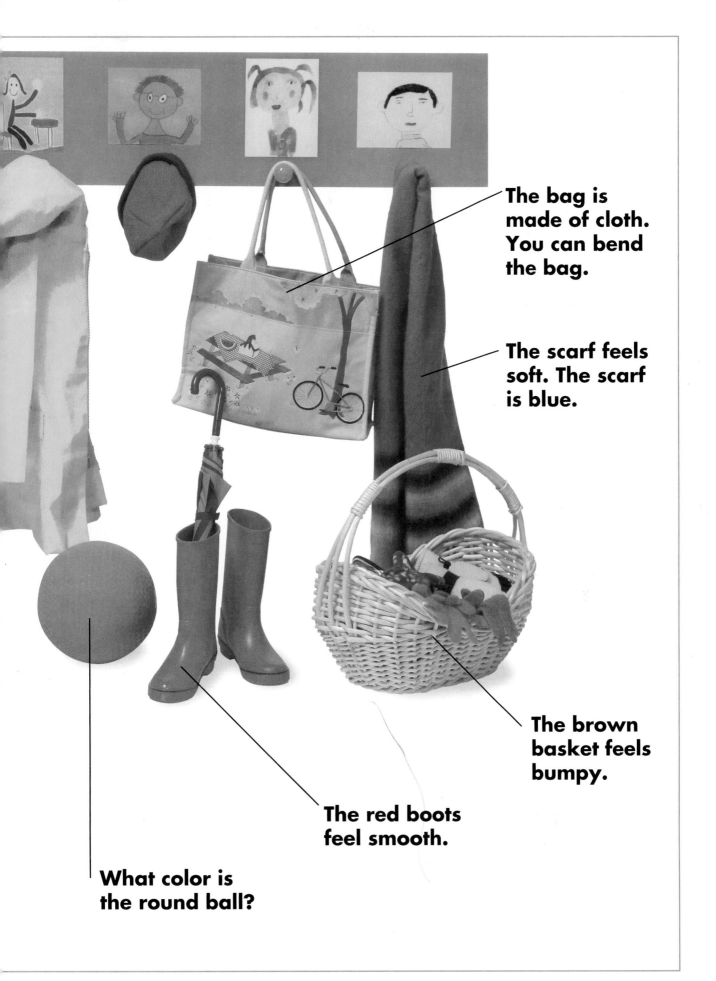

The bag is made of cloth. You can bend the bag.

The scarf feels soft. The scarf is blue.

The brown basket feels bumpy.

The red boots feel smooth.

What color is the round ball?

Lesson 2

What are solids, liquids, and gases?

What toys do you see?
All of the toys are solids.

A **solid** takes up space.
A solid has its own shape.
A solid does not change shape
when it is moved from place to place.

**What colors
are the blocks?
What shapes
are the blocks?**

1. ✓Checkpoint What is a solid?

2. 🎯 Choose two solids from the picture.
How are the solids **alike and different**?

Liquids and Gases

A liquid can change shape.
A **liquid** takes the shape of
its container.
A liquid takes up space.
A liquid is matter.

**Look at the
different shapes
a liquid can take.**

A **gas** can change size and shape. Gas takes up space. Gas takes the shape of the container it fills.

Gas takes the size and shape of the ball.

Air is a gas.
Air is all around us.
Air is matter.

The bubbles are filled with air.

✓ **Lesson Checkpoint**

1. What is one way to group the matter on these pages?

2. How are solids and liquids **alike and different**?

Lesson 3

How does matter change?

Matter can be changed in many different ways. Look at how things in the picture have changed.

A whole apple has one shape. Apples can be cut into new shapes.

The straw was straight. Now it is bent.

The shape of the bread changed.

A liquid can be cooled until it freezes.
A solid can be heated until it melts.
Find something in the picture that
is melting.

Hurry!
**Put the popsicle
in the cooler.**

**The popsicle
is melting.**

1. ✓ Checkpoint How can
matter be changed?

2. How are the whole
apple and the cut apple
alike and different?

Mixing Solids and Liquids

You can mix different kinds of matter. Look at the soup in the picture. The soup is made of different solids and a liquid.

The solids are mixed with the liquid. You can take the solids out of the liquid.

The carrots are solids.

The noodles are solids.

The chicken is a solid.

The broth is a liquid.

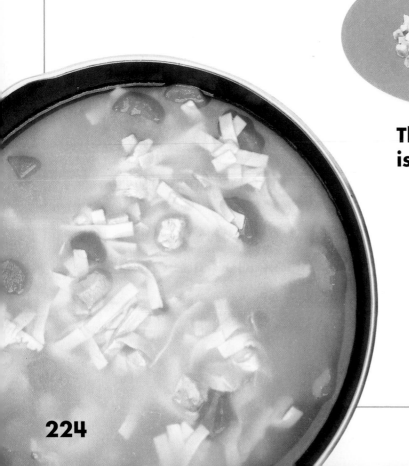

Some solids dissolve in liquids. **Dissolve** means to spread throughout a liquid.

The salt will dissolve in the water.
This makes salt water.

✔ **Lesson Checkpoint**

1. What happens when a solid dissolves?

2. **Writing** in Science Tell what solids you might put in a salad. Tell what liquid you might mix with your salad.

Lesson 4

How can water change?

Water is a liquid.
Water freezes when it gets very cold.
The water changes to ice.

Ice is a solid.
Heat melts ice.
The ice changes to water.

**Ice is frozen water.
Ice feels cold
and hard.**

Water boils when it gets very hot.
Heat changes the water to a gas
called water vapor.
You cannot see water vapor.

The water inside the pot is boiling. Steam is coming out of the pot. Steam is water vapor that is given off when water boils.

1. 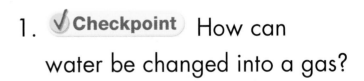 How can water be changed into a gas?

2. **Technology** in Science   What do people use to boil water?

Water Can Evaporate

Everything got wet.
What will happen to the water?

Some of the water on the ground will evaporate. **Evaporate** means to change from a liquid to a gas.

The water on the ground can change to water vapor.

Water in an open container will disappear. Water in a closed container will not disappear.

Heat from sunlight causes the water in the puddle to evaporate.

✓**Lesson Checkpoint**

1. What happens to water that evaporates?

2. **Writing** in Science In your **science journal,** write about what will happen to a puddle on a hot day.

229

Lesson 5

What are other ways matter changes?

Sometimes one kind of matter changes into a different kind of matter. It will not change back to the way it was.

The table and chairs are made of iron. The picture shows that part of the table has changed to rust.

The apple has changed color inside. The apple's color will not change back.

Paper can burn.
Paper changes into ashes when it burns.
Ashes will not change back into paper.

People can use paper to start a campfire.

The paper will burn.

The paper turns into ashes when it is burned.

✓**Lesson Checkpoint**

1. How can paper change?

2. **Math** in Science Suppose you had three apples. Each apple was cut into two pieces. How many pieces of apple would you have? Write a number sentence.

231

Investigate Will it float or sink?

Materials

classroom objects

tub with water

What to Do

1 Choose an object.

2 **Predict** Will it float or sink?

3 Put the object in the water. Does it float or sink?

Be careful!

Clean up spills right away.

Process Skills

When you **classify**, you sort things that are alike and different.

4 Try the other objects.

5 Collect data in the chart.

Sink or Float?		
Object	**Predict**	**What happens?**
eraser	float	sink

Explain Your Results

1. **Classify** Which objects float and which objects sink?
2. Why do you think some objects float and others sink?

Go Further
Would the same objects float or sink in salt water? Try it and find out.

Comparing Height and Weight

Orange juice is a liquid. The cup, the bottle, and the jug all hold orange juice. Compare their heights.

List the bottle, cup, and jug in order from tallest to shortest.

Bottle   **Cup**   **Jug**

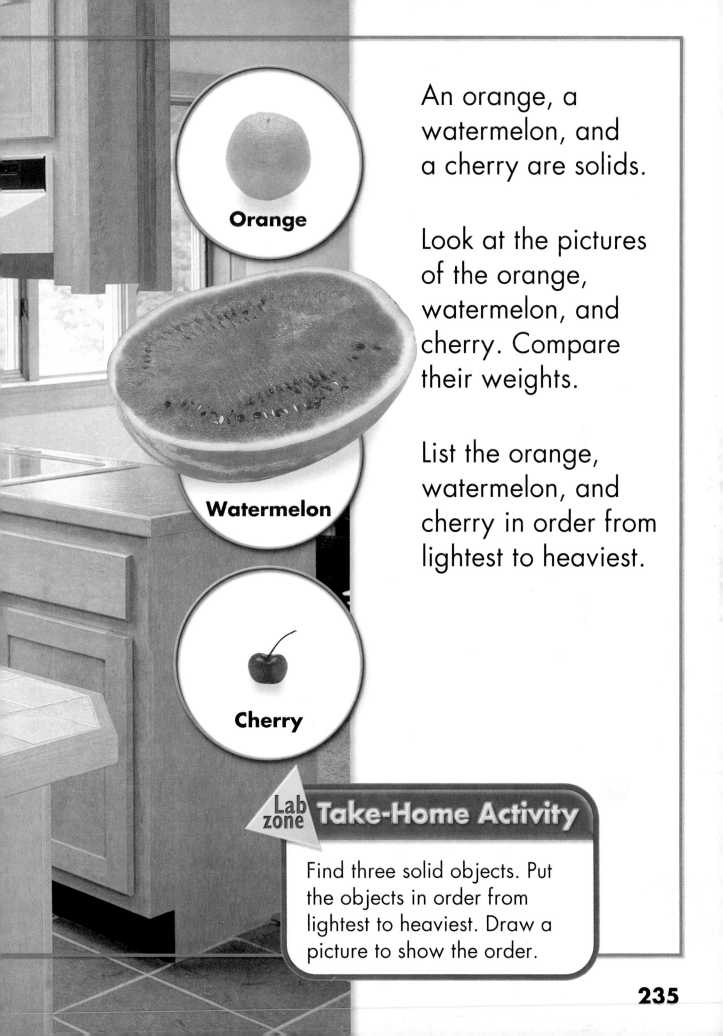

Orange

Watermelon

Cherry

An orange, a watermelon, and a cherry are solids.

Look at the pictures of the orange, watermelon, and cherry. Compare their weights.

List the orange, watermelon, and cherry in order from lightest to heaviest.

Lab zone Take-Home Activity

Find three solid objects. Put the objects in order from lightest to heaviest. Draw a picture to show the order.

235

Vocabulary

Which picture goes with each word?

1. solid

2. liquid

3. gas

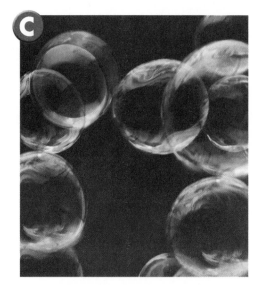

What did you learn?

4. How are solids and liquids alike and different?

5. Look around you. Name an object you can see. What are three ways to describe it?

6. What are four ways matter can change?

7. Classify Take five objects out of your desk. What is one way you can group the objects? Now group them in a different way.

Alike and Different

Alike	Different

8. How are the balls **alike and different**?

Test Prep

Fill in the circle next to the correct answer.

9. What happens to water when it boils?

ⓐ It changes to a solid.

ⓑ It changes to a gas.

ⓒ It changes to a liquid.

ⓓ It dissolves.

10. Writing in Science Write a sentence. Tell what happens when you mix salt and water.

Matter on the Moon

Look up in the sky at night.
You can see the Moon.
Astronauts from NASA
have walked on the Moon.

Matter weighs more on
Earth than on the Moon.

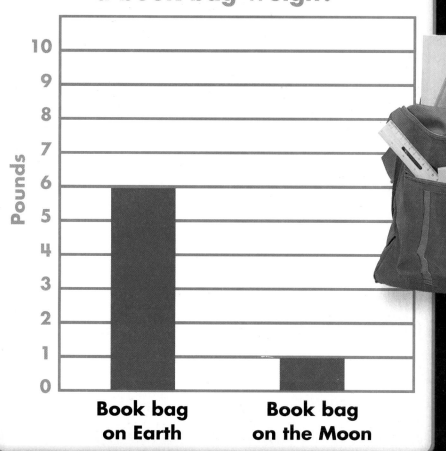

How many pounds does a book bag weigh?

Pounds

10	
9	
8	
7	
6	
5	
4	
3	
2	
1	
0	

Book bag on Earth   **Book bag on the Moon**

Lab zone Take-Home Activity

Draw a picture of yourself on the Moon. Show your picture to your family. Tell them if you would weigh more or less on the Moon.

Blowing Glass

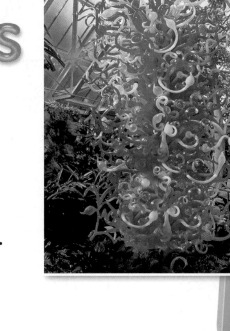

Read Together

Glass is a solid.
Fire can change glass.
Glass melts when it gets very hot!
Fire makes glass very hot and soft.

Glassblowers use glass to make
things such as bowls and vases.
Glassblowers put hot glass at one
end of a long tube.
They blow into the other end.
Then they use tools to shape the glass.

**Dale Chihuly is
a glassblower.**

Lab zone Take-Home Activity

Place a balloon on one
end of a cardboard tube.
Use tape to hold it in place.
Blow into the other end of
the tube. Describe what
happens to your balloon.

EC NTL 10 9 8 7 6 5 4

You Will Discover
- different ways that things move.
- how sounds are made.

Chapter 9
Movement and Sound

online
Student Edition
sfsuccessnet.com

What makes objects move?

force

gravity

speed

magnet

attract

S   N   S   N

pole

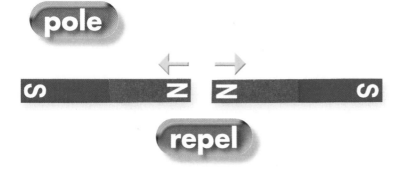

repel

vibrate

Vibrate means to move back and forth very fast.

243

Be careful!

Wear your safety goggles.

Explore How can you move the car?

Materials

safety goggles

rubber band

2 pencils

toy car

What to Do

1 Have your partners stretch a rubber band between 2 pencils.

2 Put the car next to the rubber band.

3 Pull the rubber band back. Let go. Observe.

What pushes the car?

Hold each pencil in place.

Process Skills

Predict means to tell what you think might happen.

Explain Your Results
Predict What would happen if you pulled the rubber band farther back?

Cause and Effect

A cause is why something happens. An effect is what happens.

Science Story

Moving a Wagon

The girl can use the wagon to move her toy.

Apply It!

Suppose the girl starts pulling the wagon. **Predict** what effect that will have on the wagon.

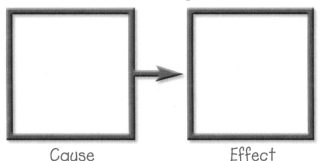

Cause   Effect

♪ Pull the Sled!

Sung to the tune of "Three Blind Mice"
Lyrics by Gerri Brioso & Richard Freitas/The Dovetail Group, Inc.

Pull the sled.

Pull the sled.

Pull it up the hill.

Pull it up the hill.

Don't let go or you soon will see

The sled sliding down 'cause of gravity.

To get it back up you must certainly,

Pull the sled!

246

What makes things move?

The children use force to move the sled to the top of the hill.

Force is a push or a pull that may make something move.

Suppose the children let go of the sled.

Whoosh! Gravity pulls the sled down the hill. **Gravity** is a force that pulls things toward the ground.

Using Force

The children use force to move the sleds. The children use a little force to pull the sleds over the snow.

Snow can be very heavy. Look at the girl in the picture below. The girl uses a lot of force to move the heavy snow.

Suppose the girl drops the shovel. Gravity will pull it to the ground.

These children pull the sleds to move them over the snow.

✔️ Lesson Checkpoint

1. What is gravity?

2. **Writing** in Science Write in your **science journal.** Tell how the children use force to make the sled move.

249

Lesson 2

What is speed?

Force can change the way things move. The child pushes the car with a lot of force. The car moves quickly.

The car has a lot of speed. **Speed** is how quickly or slowly something moves.

The child pushes the car with less force. The car will move at a slower speed.

√ **Lesson Checkpoint**

1. What is speed?

2. **Cause and Effect** What causes the car to have a lot of speed?

The boy pushes the car.

The car slows down.
The car stops.

The girl can push the car in another direction.

Lesson 3

How do things move?

Things can move up and down.
Things can move left and right.
Things can move in a straight
line or in a circle.

Things can even
move in a zigzag.
How do the things
in these pictures move?

First, the marble rolls down the orange bar. Then, it zigzags down the other bars.

The shiny balls move back and forth.

The cars follow the path of the track.
First, the cars move around one curve.
Next, the cars go straight.
Then, the cars move around
another curve.

The cars go around and around the track.

1. ✓**Checkpoint** What are some ways things can move?

2. **Math** in Science Count how many bars the marble will roll down.

Different Places

Look at the block tower.
Find the long red block.
How many blocks are above
the red block?
How many blocks are below
the red block?

Find the block next to the tower.
What color is the block?

**This orange block
is between two
yellow blocks.**

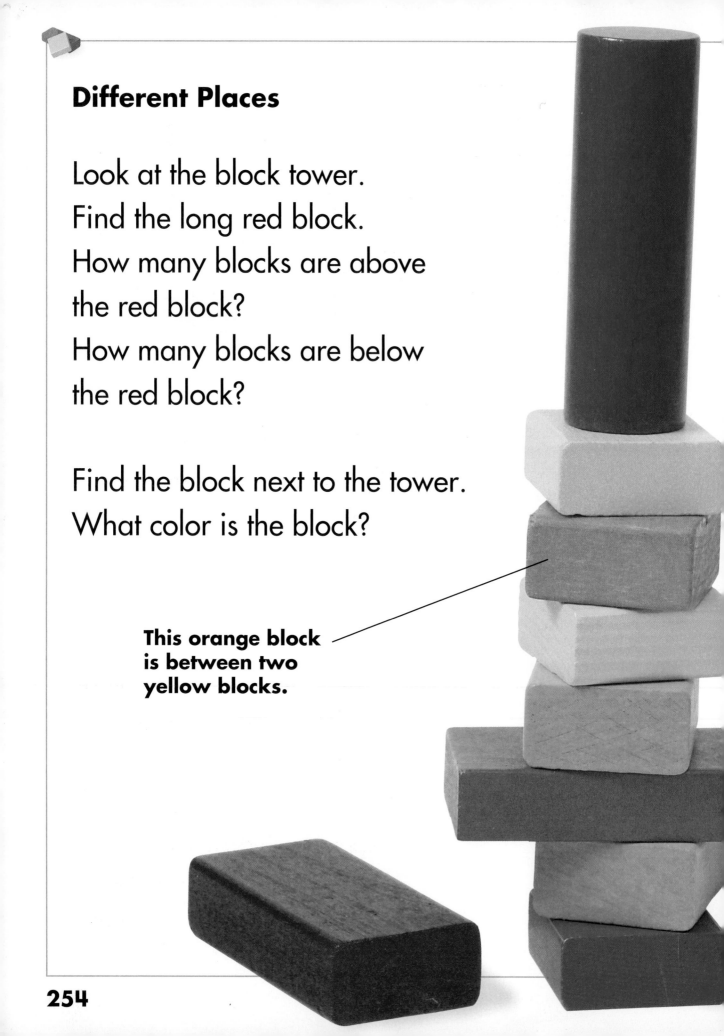

Crash!

Look at what can happen if you pull out the bottom block.

✓**Lesson Checkpoint**

1. Write in your **science journal.** Tell what is above you, below you, and next to you.

2. **Cause and Effect** Suppose you move the orange block in the tower. How might this affect the blocks next to the orange block?

What do magnets do?

What holds the train cars together?
Magnets do!

A **magnet** is an object that
attracts some kinds of metal.
Attract means to pull toward.

N stands for
north pole.
S stands for
south pole.

A magnet has two poles.
A **pole** is at the end of some magnets.
Every magnet has a north pole
and a south pole.

Different poles attract
each other. A north
pole and a south pole
attract each other.

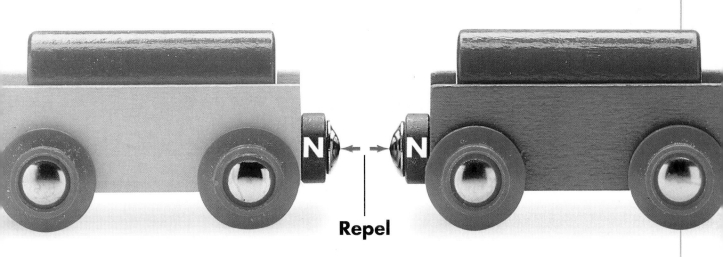

Repel

Suppose you turn one train car around.
Now two north poles are by each other.
The two north poles repel each other.
Repel means to push away.
Poles that are the same will repel each other.

1. ✓**Checkpoint** When do magnets attract
each other?

2. **Writing** in Science Write a sentence. Tell what
will happen if you put two south poles together.

Pulling Metal

Look at the objects in the basket.
What will the magnet attract?
The magnet will attract things
made of iron.
Iron is one kind of metal.

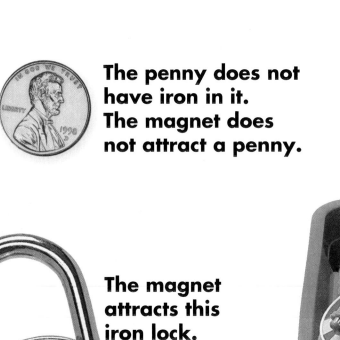

The penny does not
have iron in it.
The magnet does
not attract a penny.

The magnet
attracts this
iron lock.

A magnet can pull on an object made of iron without touching it. The magnet pulls more on an object when it is close to the object.

The magnet will not attract this plastic pail.

✔ Lesson Checkpoint

1. What is one way to find out if something has iron in it?

2. Writing in Science Write in your **science journal.** Make a list of ways that people use magnets.

Lesson 5

How are sounds made?

When a sound is made something vibrates. **Vibrate** means to move back and forth very fast.

Gently pluck a string on the banjo. It sounds soft. Pluck the string harder. Now it sounds loud.

Parts of the banjo vibrate when you pluck the strings. The vibrating parts make sounds.

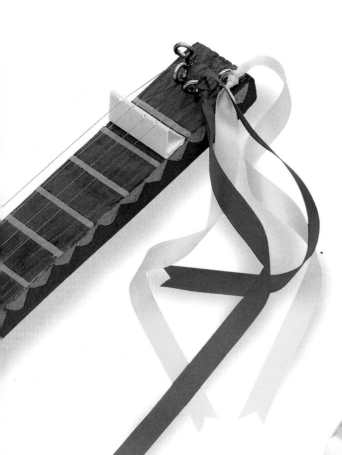

Give the top of the drum a gentle tap. The top of the drum will vibrate. The top of the drum will make a soft sound.

✓ Lesson Checkpoint

1. How does a banjo make a sound?

2. **Health** in Science Loud sounds can hurt your ears. What might you do to protect your ears?

261

Lesson 6

What sounds are around us?

Suppose you were on this street. What sounds might you hear?

You might hear sirens.
You might hear honks.
You might hear beeps.

Honks, beeps, and sirens tell us to be careful.

Zoom!
Look up! What makes that sound in the sky?

1. ✓Checkpoint Describe two sounds that can help you.

2. Technology in Science Name three machines and the sounds they make.

Sounds of Nature

Many things in nature make sounds.
Look at these pictures.
What sounds might you hear?

✓ **Lesson Checkpoint**

1. What sounds in nature might be loud?

2. **Social Studies** in Science   What sounds might you hear in your neighborhood?

Chirp! Chirp!

That chirping sounds like baby birds.

Clap!
That loud clap
sounds like thunder.

How might
the falling
water
sound?

Crash!
That crashing
sounds like
waves hitting
the rocks.

How might
falling leaves
sound?

Investigate What do you hear?

Materials

safety goggles

plastic cup and rubber band

paper cup with hole in bottom

string and paper clip

cup with water

What to Do

1 Make your first noisemaker. Stretch a rubber band around the plastic cup.

2 Hold the bottom of the cup to your ear. Pluck the rubber band gently. Listen. Record what you hear.

Be careful!

Wear your goggles!

3 Make your second noisemaker. Push the string through the hole in the cup.

4 Tie the paper clip on the outside of the cup. Wet the string.

5 Hold the cup. Pull down on the wet string with your fingers. Listen. Record what you hear.

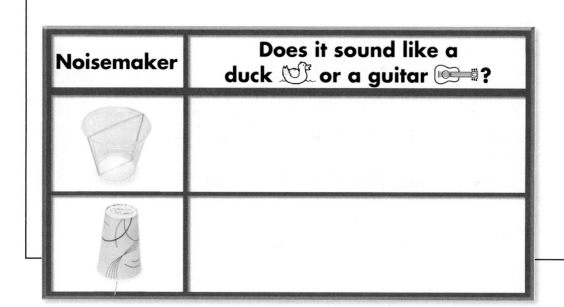

Noisemaker	Does it sound like a duck or a guitar?

Explain Your Results

1. **Infer** Why do you think you hear the different sounds?

2. What instruments do you know that vibrate?

Go Further

What sound would you hear if you use a dry string? Try it and find out.

Speed

Moving At Different Speeds

slowest ➡ slower ➡ slow

Use the pictures to answer the questions.
1. What two things are faster than a car?
2. What is slower than a turtle?

fast ➡ **faster** ➡ **fastest**

Lab zone **Take-Home Activity**

Find pictures of six things that move. Put them in order from slowest to fastest.

Vocabulary

Which picture goes with each word?

1. attract

2. pole

3. repel

What did you learn?

4. What makes things move?

5. What force pulls things toward the ground?

6. What are three different ways that things can move?

7. What is speed?

8. How are sounds made?

9. **Infer** What might happen if you hit the top of a drum hard?

Cause and Effect

10. You cause a bike to move by pushing the pedals. Suppose you push harder. What effect will that have on how the bike moves?

Cause	Effect

 **Test Prep**

Fill in the circle next to the correct answer.

11. What happens to magnets if you try to touch their south poles to each other?
    Ⓐ They attract.
    Ⓑ They vibrate.
    Ⓒ They repel.
    Ⓓ They pull.

12. **Writing** in Science Write two sentences. Tell what happens when magnets attract and repel some things.

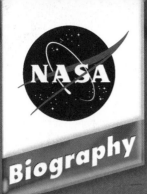

Dr. Shamim Rahman

Read Together

Shamim Rahman was six years old when he saw an astronaut walk on the moon. Since then, he has always wanted to be a rocket scientist.

Now Dr. Rahman is a rocket scientist at NASA. Rockets help the space shuttle move into space. Dr. Rahman works to build and test newer and better rockets.

Dr. Rahman is on a team that checks the rocket engines before the shuttle takes off.

Lab zone Take-Home Activity

Scientists send rockets into space to take pictures of Earth. Draw what you think Earth would look like from space. Explain your picture to your family.

272

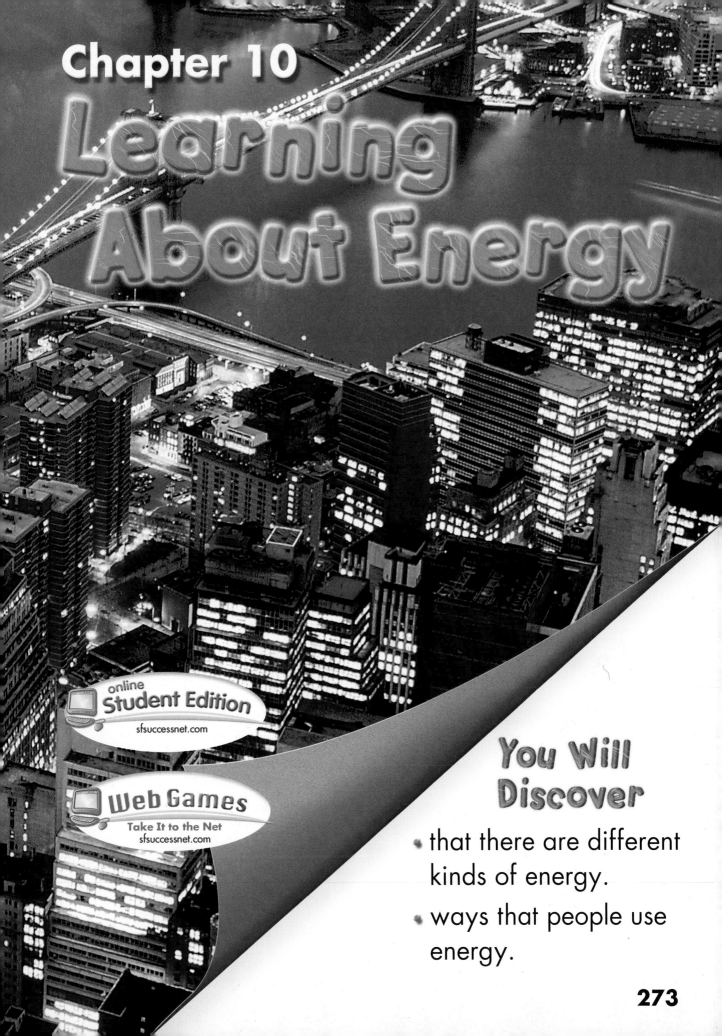

Chapter 10
Learning About Energy

online
Student Edition
sfsuccessnet.com

Web Games
Take It to the Net
sfsuccessnet.com

You Will Discover

- that there are different kinds of energy.
- ways that people use energy.

Where does energy come from?

energy

heat

shadow

fuel

274

electricity

battery

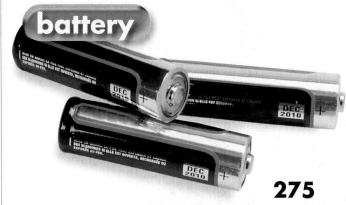

Explore Can the Sun's light heat water?

Materials

2 thermometers

2 cups with cold water

temperature chart

red crayons

Process Skills

You **infer** when you draw a conclusion to answer a question.

What to Do

1 Put 1 thermometer in each cup. Record the temperatures.

2 Put 1 cup in a sunny place. Put the other cup in a shady place.

3 Wait 2 hours. Record the temperatures on your temperature chart.

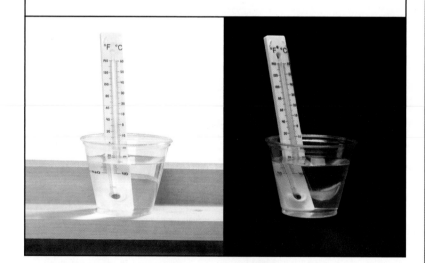

Explain Your Results

Infer Why did one cup have warmer water after 2 hours?

How to Read Science

Draw Conclusions

You draw conclusions when you decide something about what you see and read.

Science Story

Playing Outside

The Sun gives Mark light to read.
It is now late in the day.
Mark turns on the light.

Apply It!
Infer Why does Mark turn on the light?

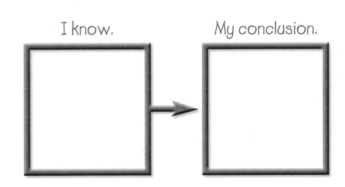

I know.

My conclusion.

You Are There

Energy

Sung to the tune of "My Bonnie"
Lyrics by Gerri Brioso & Richard Freitas/The Dovetail Group, Inc.

I sit on the beach in the summer.
The sun is up high in the sky.
The light from the sun heats
the beach sand.
Just ask me and I'll tell you why.

Science Songs

Lesson 1

What gives off heat?

What a hot day!
Heat comes from the light of the Sun.
Heat moves from warmer places to cooler places.
Heat moves from warmer objects to cooler objects.

Light from the Sun warms the land.
Light from the Sun warms the water.
Light from the Sun warms the air.

Heat

Look at the picture.
Heat comes from the fire.
The heat warms the food.
The heat warms the air.

**Fire was used
to heat the
marshmallow.**

The girl is drinking hot cocoa to warm up. Heat comes from the hot cocoa.

Rub your hands together.
Rubbing things together makes heat.
The heat from rubbing your hands together makes them warm.

Heat comes from other things too.
Heat comes from lamps, stoves, and toasters.
What else can give off heat?

✓ **Lesson Checkpoint**

1. What are five things that heat comes from?

2. 🎯 **Draw Conclusions** What would happen to Earth without the Sun?

What can energy do?

Light is a form of energy. **Energy** can change things. Energy from the Sun can change the temperature.

The thermometers show that the black towel is warmer than the white towel.

Energy from the Sun can change things.

Things with lighter colors feel cooler than things with darker colors.

In summer, many people like to wear clothes with lighter colors. Lighter colors take in less energy from the Sun.

✓ **Lesson Checkpoint**

1. What can energy from the Sun do?

2. 🔄 **Draw Conclusions** What color could you wear to stay cool on a sunny summer day?

Lesson 3

What makes light and shadows?

Look at the light around you.
Is the light from the Sun?
Is the light from a fire?

Light comes from both of these things.
Light comes from stars and candles too.
Where else does light come from?

Light can shine through thin colored paper.

Light comes from light bulbs. The light bulbs shine in the dark room.

See the firefly's light. The firefly shines in the dark.

1. ✔Checkpoint What are some things that give off light?

2. Writing in Science Write two sentences in your **science journal.** Tell about the lights you see at night.

Making Shadows

Light passes through some things.
Light will pass through a window.
Light will not pass through everything.
Light will not pass through you.

Shine the flashlight on the toy.
The toy blocks the light.
The toy makes a shadow.
A **shadow** is made
when something blocks
the light.

**Look at the shape of
the shadow. What
does it look like?**

A shadow is large when the light is close. A shadow is small when the light is far away.

1. ✓**Checkpoint** What causes a shadow?

2. **Art** in Science Make a shadow on white paper. Have a friend trace the shadow.

morning

Look at the tree's shadow in the morning.

noon

Look at the shadow at noon. The shadow is shorter.

Changing Shadows

The tree blocks the Sun's light.
The tree makes a shadow.
Shadows are long when the
Sun seems low in the sky.

The Sun seems to move during the day.
The Sun is high in the sky at noon.

Look at the tree's shadow late in the day.

It is late in the day.
Now the shadow is in a different place.

✓ **Lesson Checkpoint**

1. How does a tree's shadow change from morning to night?

2. **Math** in Science Measure a shadow in the morning and at noon. Which is longer?

289

Lesson 4

What uses energy around us?

Cars stop and go.
Most cars get energy from fuel.
Fuel is anything that is burned
to make heat or power.

Cars use gasoline as a fuel.
The car's engine burns the fuel.
Now the car has the energy to move.

Electricity makes street
lights work.
Electricity makes the lights
in the walk sign work too.

**The lights in the
sign change.**

SciLinks   Take It to the Net   keyword: electricity
sfsuccessnet.com   code: g1p290

Cars use fuel
to move.

The streetlight
uses electricity
to shine at night.

1. ✓Checkpoint How does
a car get energy to move?

2. Writing in Science Tell how
you use lights each day.

Using Energy

How does the fan get energy?
The fan gets energy from electricity.

Electricity moves through power
lines into a building.
Electricity moves from the outlet
through the cord.

Now the fan has energy.
Turn the fan on.
The fan blades move.

**What kind of energy
do these things use?**

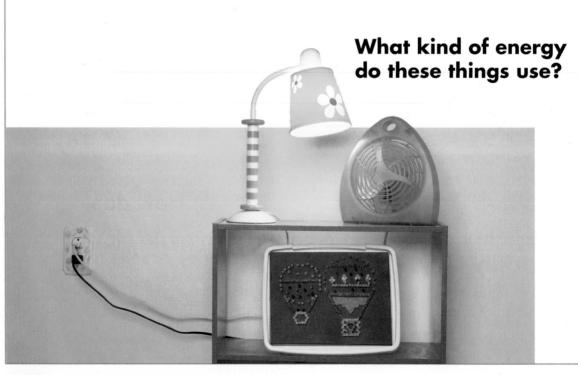

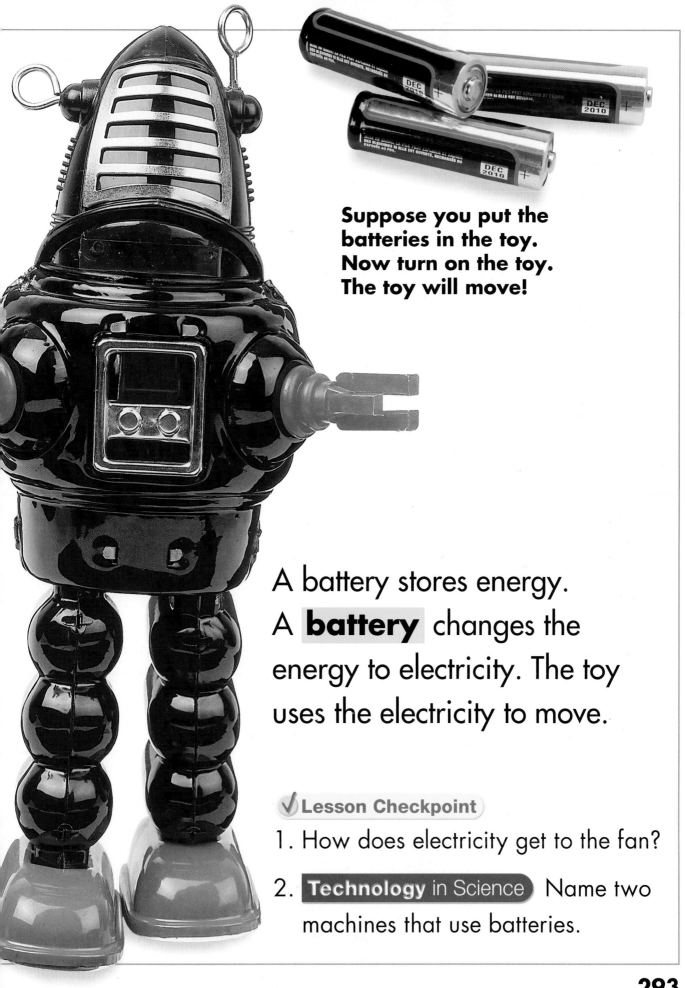

Suppose you put the batteries in the toy. Now turn on the toy. The toy will move!

A battery stores energy. A **battery** changes the energy to electricity. The toy uses the electricity to move.

✓ Lesson Checkpoint

1. How does electricity get to the fan?

2. **Technology** in Science Name two machines that use batteries.

Lesson 5

How do you get energy?

Yum! What foods do you see?
You get energy from food.
You need energy to move.
You need energy to grow and change.

milk

cheese

**Milk and cheese help
you grow strong teeth
and bones.**

fruit

**Bread and
cereal give
you energy
to play.**

bread and cereal

294

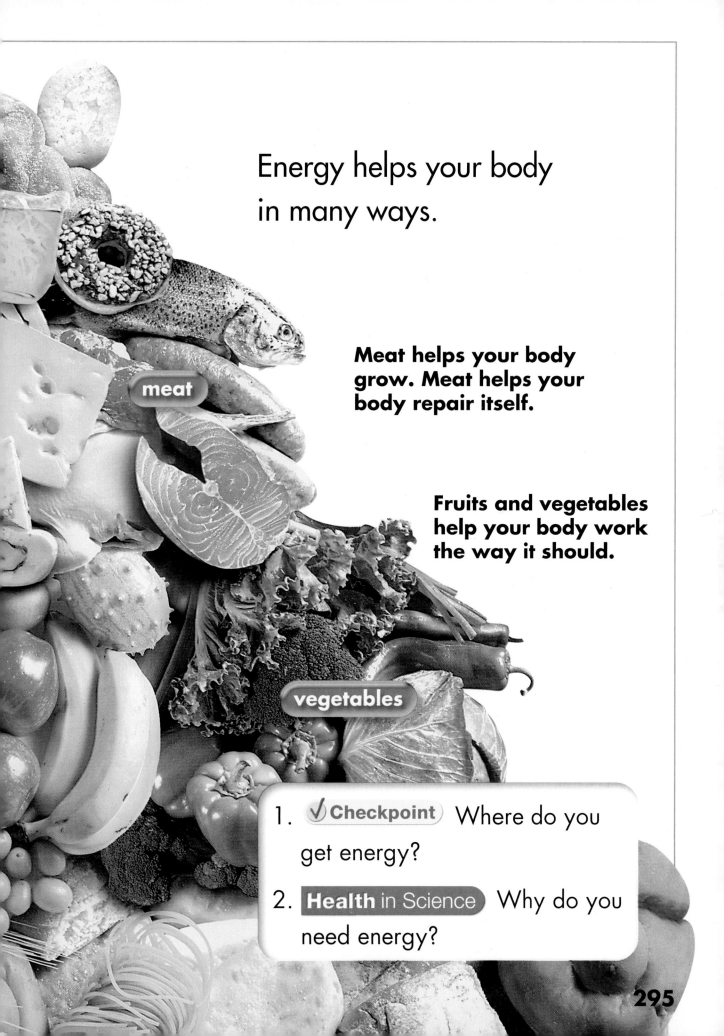

Energy helps your body in many ways.

Meat helps your body grow. Meat helps your body repair itself.

meat

Fruits and vegetables help your body work the way it should.

vegetables

1. ✓Checkpoint Where do you get energy?

2. **Health** in Science Why do you need energy?

When You Use Energy

You use energy all day long.
You use energy when you move.
You use energy when you play.

You use energy when you sit.
You use energy to turn the pages
of a book.

You even use energy when you sleep.
You need energy for everything you do.

✓ Lesson Checkpoint

1. Why do you need energy while you sleep?

2. Writing in Science In your **science journal,**
   make a list of 6 things you do that use
   energy.

You use energy
when you swim.

You think when you read.
Thinking takes energy too!

You use energy to hop
from square to square.

Your body is growing
and changing even when
you sleep. Growing and
changing take energy.

297

Merry-Go-Round

by Dorothy Baruch

I climbed up on the merry-go-round,
And it went round and round.
I climbed up on a big brown horse
And it went up and down.

Around and round
And up and down,
Around and round
And up and down
I sat high up
On a big brown horse
And rode around
On the merry-go-round.

Discovery CHANNEL SCHOOL™ Science Fair Projects

Idea 1

Energy in an Aquarium

Plan a project.

Find out how the light from the Sun can change the water in an aquarium.

Idea 2

Energy in a Terrarium

Plan a project.

Find out how animals in a terrarium get energy.

Using Scientific Methods

1. Ask a question.
2. Make a hypothesis.
3. Plan a fair test.
4. Do your test.
5. Record and collect data.
6. Tell your conclusion.
7. Go further.

Science Fair **Central** More science fair help
sfsuccessnet.com

EC NTL 10 9 8 7 6 5 4

Unit D

Space and Technology

Chapter 11
Day and Night Sky

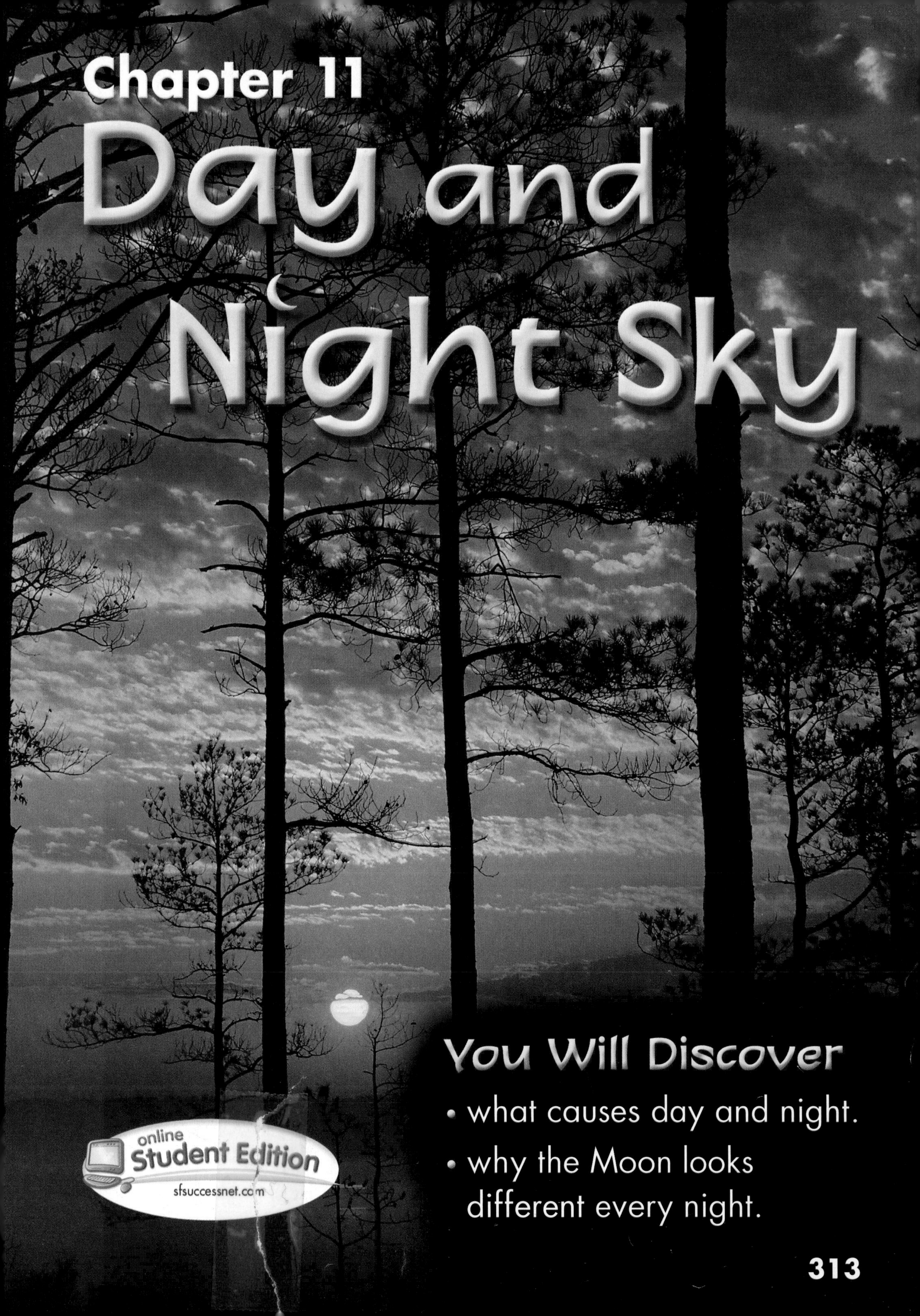

You Will Discover

- what causes day and night.
- why the Moon looks different every night.

online
Student Edition
sfsuccessnet.com

What is in the sky?

Sun

star

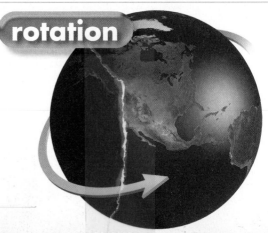

rotation

314

Moon

planet

telescope

315

Explore Why does the Sun look small?

Materials

ruler

paper plate

What to Do

1 Measure across a plate. Label the plate **Sun**.

2 Have your partner hold the plate.

3 Move 5 steps away from your partner.

4 Hold the ruler in front of you. Close one eye. Measure again.

Sun

Explain Your Results
Communicate What seems to happen to the size of the plate when you move away?

Reading Skills

Important Details

Important details are pictures and words that tell you something.

Science Story

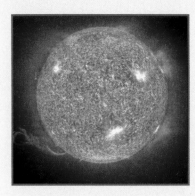

The Sun

Look at the picture of the Sun.
We get light from the Sun.
The Sun is very far from Earth.
You can see the Sun in the
day sky.

Apply It!

Communicate List three important details you saw and read about the Sun.

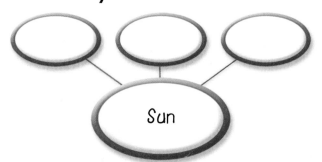

Sun

Look Up High!

Sung to the tune of "This Old Man"
Lyrics by Gerri Brioso & Richard Freitas/The Dovetail Group, Inc.

The daytime sky, the daytime sky.

What do you see in the daytime sky?

Please look up and tell me
everything you see,

In the sky above you and me.

Lesson 1

What is in the day sky?

The Sun makes
the day sky bright.
The **Sun** is a star.
A **star** is a big
ball of hot gas.

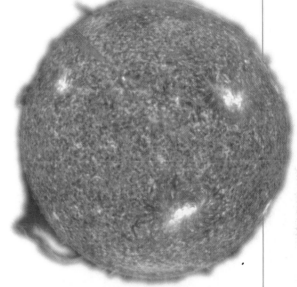

**Light from the
Sun warms Earth.**

What else do you
see in the day sky?
You may see clouds.
You may see birds.

Sometimes you can even see
the Moon in the day sky.

The Sun is low in the sky early in the day.

The Sun is above you at noon.

The Sun warms the baby lion.

Plants need sunlight to grow.

The Bright Sun

The Sun lights Earth.
Living things need light from the Sun to live and grow.

The Sun is bigger than Earth.
The Sun looks small because it is far away.

The Sun is low in the sky again late in the day.

We say that the Sun rises and sets, but really it does not. The Sun looks like it is moving because Earth is moving.

✓ Lesson Checkpoint

1. Why does the Sun look small?

2. **Writing** in Science   Write in your **science journal.** Tell about the Sun.

What causes day and night?

Earth is always moving.
Earth turns around and around.
This is called **rotation.**
Earth makes one rotation every day.

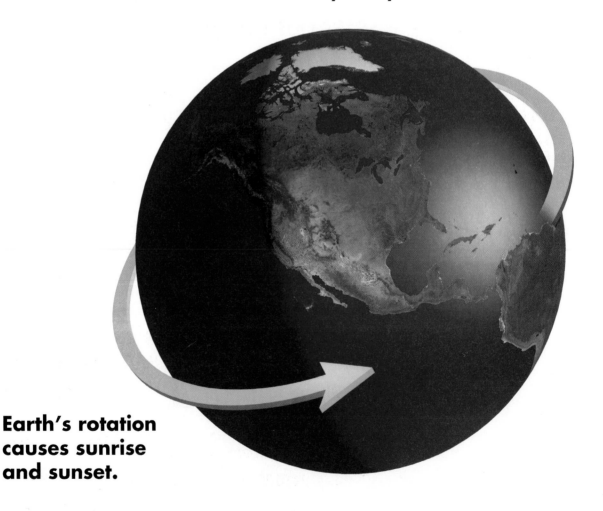

Earth's rotation causes sunrise and sunset.

It is night when your part of the world faces away from the Sun.

It is day when your part of Earth faces the Sun. Earth's rotation causes day and night.

It is night in Tokyo when it is day in Chicago.

It is day in Chicago when it is night in Tokyo.

✓ Lesson Checkpoint

1. How often does Earth make one rotation?

2. **Math** in Science   What comes next in the pattern below?
day, night, day, night, day, _____

Lesson 3

What is in the night sky?

The sky is filled with many stars.
Most stars can be seen only at night.
Stars give off light.
Stars seem to move across the night sky.

Earth is a **planet.**
Planets do not give off light.
Planets move around the Sun.

You might use a telescope
to see things in the sky.
A **telescope** makes things
that are far away look closer.

A telescope makes things look bigger or brighter.

Stars look tiny because they are far away. The Sun is the closest star to Earth.

Saturn, Mars, and Venus are planets. Sometimes you can see these planets in the night sky.

1. ✓Checkpoint How does a telescope help us look at things in the sky?

2. 🎯 **Important Details** Name planets you might see in the night sky.

The Moon at Night

The **Moon** moves around Earth. The Moon looks small because it is far away.

The Moon is round.

The Moon is not like Earth.
The Moon has no air.
The Moon has no animals.
The Moon has no plants.

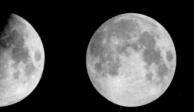

This is what the Moon looks like at different times.

The Sun's light shines on the Moon. You only see the part of the Moon lit by the Sun.

The part of the moon lit by the Sun changes each night. The Moon looks a little different each night. The Moon looks the same again about every 29 days.

✓Lesson Checkpoint

1. How long does it take for the Moon to look the same again?

2. 🎯 What is one **important detail** you saw or read about the Moon?

327

Investigate Why can you see things in the night sky?

Materials

shoe box viewer

star and ball

flashlight

clay

What to Do

1 **Make a model** of the night sky.

2 Put the star in the clay. Put the lid on the box. Observe.

Look through this hole.

This star is like a real star.

3 Take out the star. Put the ball on the clay. Put the lid on the box.

The ball is like the Moon.

Look through this hole.

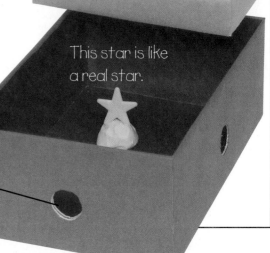

Process Skills

Investigate to learn why you can see things in the night sky.

4 Shine the flashlight through the side hole. Observe.

The flashlight is like the Sun.

Look through this hole.

	Did you need a flashlight to see it? yes or no
Ball	
Star	

Explain Your Results

1. Why can you see the star in the dark?
2. **Infer** Why can you see the Moon in the night sky?

Go Further

How could you show that the Moon can sometimes be seen in the day sky? **Investigate** to find out.

Reading a Calendar

Look at the calendar.
The calendar shows how the Moon looks
in the sky at different times of the month.

May

Sunday	Monday	Tuesday	Wednesday	Thursday	Friday	Saturday
				New Moon 1	2	3
4	5	6	7	First quarter 8	9	10
11	12	13	14	Full Moon 15	16	17
18	19	20	21	22	Third Quarter 23	24
25	26	27	28	29	New Moon 30	31

Use the calendar to answer the questions.
1. How many days are there from the new Moon to the first quarter Moon?
2. How many days are there from the new Moon to the full Moon?

Lab zone **Take-Home Activity**

Look for the Moon in the sky tonight. Estimate how many days until there will be a new Moon.

Vocabulary

Which picture goes with each word?

1. Moon
2. Sun
3. telescope
4. planet

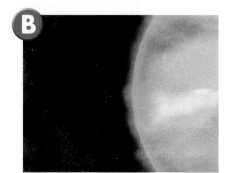

What did you learn?

5. What causes night and day?

6. What can you see in the night sky?

7. How does a telescope help you see the Moon?

8. Infer Why does it feel cooler on Earth when there are many clouds in the sky?

The Moon

Look at the picture of the Moon. The Moon is in the night sky. Part of the Moon is lit by the Sun's light.

Important Details

9. List two **important details** you saw or read about the Moon.

Moon

Test Prep

Fill in the circle next to the correct answer.

10. Which of these gives off light?

Ⓐ the Moon

Ⓑ Earth

Ⓒ a planet

Ⓓ a star

11. Writing in Science Think about Earth and the Moon. Write how they are alike and different.

Exploring the Sky

A time line shows when things happened. Look at this time line.

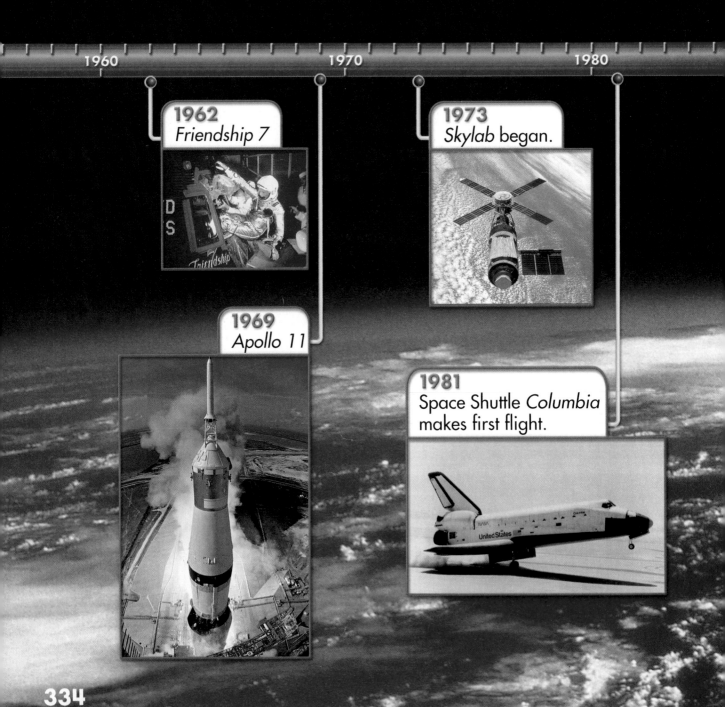

1960 — 1970 — 1980

1962
Friendship 7

1969
Apollo 11

1973
Skylab began.

1981
Space Shuttle *Columbia* makes first flight.

The pictures on these two pages show ways that NASA learns about space. These machines help NASA get information about space. These machines help NASA do experiments.

1990   2000   2004   2010

1998
International Space Station assembly began.

2004
Spirit Rover lands on Mars.

Lab
zone **Take-Home Activity**

Draw a time line that shows what has happened in your life. Share it with your family.

Astronauts

Read Together

Astronauts go into space in space shuttles.
Astronauts do work in space.
Astonauts do science experiments in space.
Astronauts fix things in space.
Astronauts take pictures in space. Astronauts need special training to work in space.

Stephanie Wilson is an astronaut. She is a mission specialist with NASA.

Lab zone Take-Home Activity

Draw a picture of yourself as an astronaut working in space. Tell what kind of work you might do in space.

ECNTL 10 9 8 7 6 5 4

Chapter 12
Science in Our World

Discovery Channel School
Student DVD

online
Student Edition
sfsuccessnet.com

You Will Discover

- what tools and machines are used to farm and build.
- that tools and machines are used to communicate.

How does technology help people?

technology

simple machine

wheel and axle

wedge

inclined plane

pulley

screw

lever

339

Technology Helps

Sung to the tune of "On Top of Old Smokey"
Lyrics by Gerri Brioso & Richard Freitas/The Dovetail Group, Inc.

Technology helps all
The farmers I know,
To make their work easier
Than a long time ago.

Lesson 1

How do farmers use technology to grow food?

Some food comes from lakes or oceans.
Some food comes from forests.
Some food comes from farm animals.
Some food comes from farm crops.

Machines help farmers grow crops.
Machines are one kind of technology.
Technology is the use of scientific knowledge to solve problems.

Farmers use machines to grow wheat. Wheat is used to make bread.

Planting and Growing Corn

It is time to plant corn!
The farmer uses a plow to get
the soil ready for planting.
The plow makes the work easier.
The plow makes the work take
less time.

**The plow turns
the soil.**

The farmer uses a seed drill to plant corn seeds. The seed drill makes the work go fast. Soon all of the corn seeds are planted. Corn plants begin to grow.

A seed drill machine helps plant corn.

✓ **Lesson Checkpoint**

1. How does a plow help a farmer plant corn?

2. **Writing** in Science Make a list of foods you eat that come from a farm.

How does food get from the farm to the store?

Is the corn ready to be picked?
The farmer checks the corn.
The farmer will pick the corn
when it is ready.

First, the corn seeds grow into a corn plant.

Next, the farmer checks the corn.

The farmer uses a harvester machine to pick the corn. The corn is loaded into a truck. The truck takes the corn to the store.

✓ **Lesson Checkpoint**

1. Name two machines used to get corn from the farm to the store.

2. 🎯 **Put Things in Order** Tell how corn gets from a field to your home.

Then, the farmer uses a machine to pick the corn.

Last, you might buy the corn at the store.

What tools can you use to make dinner?

Let's get the tools we need to make dinner!
People use tools to make work easier.
Each tool helps do a different job.
Only use a knife or scissors when an
older person can help you.

Cut! Cut!
**Scissors can help you
cut tortillas for chips.**

**A grater helps you
to cut cheese into
small pieces.**

**A measuring cup can
help you get just the
right amount of cheese.**

What other tools might you use to
make tacos and salsa for dinner?

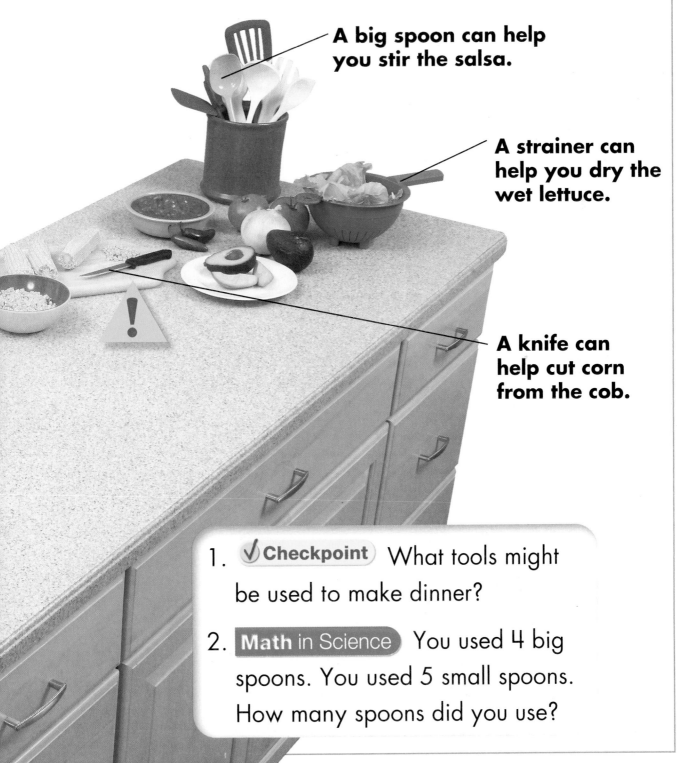

**A big spoon can help
you stir the salsa.**

**A strainer can
help you dry the
wet lettuce.**

**A knife can
help cut corn
from the cob.**

1. ✔Checkpoint What tools might
   be used to make dinner?

2. **Math** in Science You used 4 big
   spoons. You used 5 small spoons.
   How many spoons did you use?

Serving Dinner

It is dinner time! What tools do you need to serve the tacos and salsa?

A large spoon can help you lift the meat.

Tongs can help you pick up the lettuce.

Some things that you cook get hot. Always have an older person help you when something is hot. A trivet keeps the pot from burning the table.

A ladle is a big, deep spoon. A ladle can help you get some salsa.

A spatula can help you lift hot tortillas off the pan.

✓**Lesson Checkpoint**

1. What are three tools used to serve dinner?

2. **Technology** in Science Draw a tool you use in the kitchen. Tell how it helps you do work.

Lesson 4

How do builders get wood for a house?

Technology changes over time.

Long ago loggers used an ax to cut down trees. Now loggers use a machine called a tree shears to cut down trees.

A tree shears makes cutting trees easier.

The logs are heavy. Long ago some loggers used animals to move the logs. Now loggers use a grappler to move the logs.

1. ✓Checkpoint What machine does a logger use to cut down trees today?

2. Technology in Science How does a grappler help loggers?

A grappler makes moving logs easier.

353

Moving Logs to the Sawmill

The heavy logs need to be loaded
onto the truck.

Look at the long-armed knuckle
boom machine!
The long arm grabs the heavy logs.
Then the machine loads the logs
onto the truck.

**First, the long-armed
knuckle boom loads
the logs onto the truck.**

**Next, the truck takes
the logs to the sawmill.**

When the truck is full, it takes the logs to the sawmill.

The logs are made into boards when they arrive at the sawmill.

✓ **Lesson Checkpoint**

1. Tell what happens at a sawmill.

2. 🎯 **Put Things in Order** Tell how a tree gets from the forest to a sawmill.

Then, another machine takes the bark off the logs.

Last, the logs are cut into boards. Now a builder can use them to build a house.

Lesson 5

What are simple machines?

A **simple machine** is a tool with few or no moving parts that makes work easier. People can use simple machines to do work.

A **wedge** is used to push things apart.
A wedge is a simple machine.

A **wheel and axle** is used to move things.
A wheel and axle is a simple machine.

A shovel is a wedge. The shovel pushes the soil apart.

A wheelbarrow has a wheel and axle.

SciLinks Take It to the Net
sfsuccessnet.com
keyword: simple machine
code: g1p356

Builders use many simple machines to make work easier.

1. ✓ Checkpoint How do simple machines help people?

2. Technology in Science What are some machines that have a wheel and axle?

Using Simple Machines

A screw is a simple machine. A **screw** is used to hold things together.

A lever is a simple machine. A **lever** can be used to lift something.

A pulley is a simple machine. A **pulley** uses a wheel and rope to move things up and down.

Screws hold the wood boards of the house together.

A lever helps lift the nail from the board.

Builders use a pulley to move objects.

An inclined plane helps to move things up or down.

An inclined plane is a simple machine. An **inclined plane** is high at one end and low at the other end.

✓ Lesson Checkpoint

1. What three simple machines can help lift things or move things up?

2. Writing in Science Write in your **science journal.** Tell about two simple machines that help people.

Lesson 6

What can you use to communicate?

You know that technology has changed over time.

Long ago people did not have computers, cameras, or radios to communicate. Today people have many ways to communicate.

How do you communicate with other people?

Hurry!
Computers tell the firefighters where to go.

Click!
You can use a digital camera. You can use email to send the picture to a friend.

Are you at the baseball game?
No, you can listen to the
baseball game on a radio!

✓ Lesson Checkpoint

1. How do a camera and email help you communicate?

2. **Social Studies** in Science How can you use technology to hear news about people who live far away from you?

Investigate How can you build a strong bridge?

Materials

safety goggles

4 books and a ruler

10 stir sticks and 10 craft sticks

tape and note card

cup and pennies

Process Skills

Making a model can help you understand why some bridges are stronger than others.

What to Do

1 Place the books 25 centimeters apart.

Wear your goggles.

Stack the books.

2 Make a model of a bridge using stir sticks and a note card.

3 Place the bridge between the books. Place the cup on the bridge.

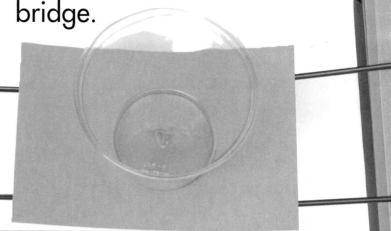

4 **Estimate** how many pennies the bridge will hold. Record.

5 Put pennies in the cup one at a time. How many pennies did the bridge hold before it fell? Record.

Which bridge is stronger?

	Number of Pennies	
	Estimate	**Count**
Stir Sticks		
Craft Sticks		

6 Try it again.
Use craft sticks.

Explain Your Results
1. How are your **models** like real bridges?
2. Explain why one bridge held more pennies than the other bridge.

Go Further
What would happen if you put the books closer together? Make a model to find the answer.

Classifying Plant Parts

Farmers use technology to grow plants.
People eat different plant parts.
People eat the seeds of corn.
People eat the roots of carrots.
People eat the leaves of spinach.
Look at the plants in the chart.

Plant Parts People Eat

Seeds	Roots	Leaves
corn	carrots	spinach
peas	beets	cabbage
lima beans	radishes	
	turnips	

Use the chart to answer these questions.
1. Does this chart show more kinds of plant seeds or plant roots that people eat?
2. Which part of a radish do people eat?

Lab zone Take-Home Activity

Make a chart like the one on this page. Draw one plant seed that you eat. Draw one plant root that you eat. Draw two plant leaves that you eat.

Vocabulary

Which picture goes with each word?

1. wheel and axle

2. wedge

3. inclined plane

4. screw

5. lever

6. pulley

What did you learn?

7. What is technology?

8. List three tools you might use to make dinner. Tell how you could use each tool.

9. List three machines used to get wood. Tell how the machines are used.

10. Communicate What is a simple machine?

Put Things in Order

11. Look at the pictures. Tell which one comes first, next, then, and last.

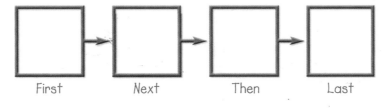

First   Next   Then   Last

Test Prep

Fill in the circle next to the correct answer.

12. Where are logs cut into boards?

Ⓐ farm

Ⓑ kitchen

Ⓒ sawmill

Ⓓ forest

13. **Writing** in Science   Write a story about two friends that use technology to communicate.

Mike Wong

Read Together

Mike Wong liked to make paper airplanes as a child. His room was full of paper airplanes. He wanted to know how airplanes flew.

Now Mike Wong works at NASA. He uses computers to find out what aircraft shapes are the best for flying. People at NASA use what they learn from Mr. Wong to make better aircraft.

Mike Wong is an aeronautical engineer.

Lab zone Take-Home Activity

Make a paper airplane. Measure how far your paper airplane can fly.

Unit D Test Talk

Write Your Answer

Read the story.

Sunlight is important to living things on Earth. Sunlight gives heat and light to Earth. Sunlight helps plants grow.

Read the question.

Why is the Sun important to living things on Earth?

Which words help you to write your answer? Write your answer.

Unit D Wrap-Up

Chapter 11

What is in the sky?
- The Sun and the Moon are in the sky.
- Stars and planets are in the sky.

Chapter 12

How does technology help people?
- Technology helps farmers grow crops.
- Technology helps people build buildings.
- Technology helps people communicate.

Performance Assessment

Make a Tool That Will Help You Work

- Make a tool that can carry things.
- Tell how your tool would make work easier.

Read More About Space and Technology!

Look for books like these in your library.

Man On The Moon
by Anastasia Suen
illustrated by Benrei Huang

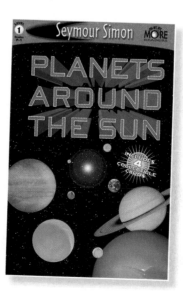

PLANETS AROUND THE SUN
Seymour Simon

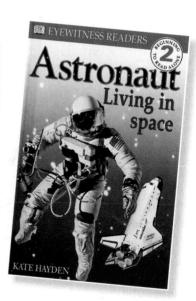

Astronaut
Living in space
KATE HAYDEN

Experiment How can a smaller person lift a bigger person on a seesaw?

A seesaw is a kind of lever. A smaller person can lift a bigger person on a seesaw. How can this happen? Experiment to find out.

Materials

eraser

ruler with cups

toy car

pennies

Process Skills

You use a **model** to find out how a seesaw moves.

Ask a question.

How can a smaller person lift a bigger person on a seesaw? Use a **model** to find out.

Make a hypothesis.

Does moving one cup closer to the middle change the number of pennies you need to lift the cup? Tell what you think.

Plan a fair test.

Make sure your cups are the same size.

Do your test.

1 Put the eraser under the ruler and cups. Put the toy in cup 1.

② Add pennies to cup 2 until cup 1 lifts up. Record how many pennies you need.

③ Take the pennies out of the cup.

④ Move cup 1 closer to the middle.

Put the eraser in the middle.

⑤ Add pennies to cup 2 until cup 1 lifts up. Record how many pennies you need.

Collect and record data.

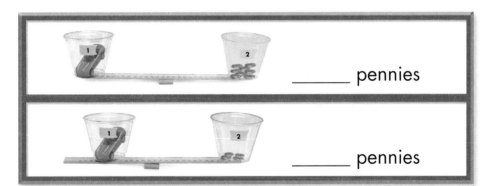

_____ pennies

_____ pennies

Tell your conclusion.
When did you use fewer pennies to lift cup 1? How can a smaller person lift a bigger person on a seesaw?

Go Further
What would happen if you added more pennies? Experiment to find out.

Taking Off

The airplane taxis down the field
And heads into the breeze,
It lifts its wheels above the ground,
It skims above the trees,

It rises higher and higher
Away up toward the sun,
It's just a speck against the sky
—And now it's gone!

Full Inquiry

Using Scientific Methods
1. Ask a question.
2. Make a hypothesis.
3. Plan a fair test.
4. Do your test.
5. Record and collect data.
6. Tell your conclusion.
7. Go further.

Idea 1

Making Paper Airplanes

Plan a project.
Find out how changing the shape of a paper airplane may change how far it flies.

Idea 2

Changing a Wheel

Plan a project.
Find out how changing the size of the wagon's wheels may improve how the wagon rolls.

EC NTL 10 9 8 7 6 5 4

Metric and Customary Measurement

Science uses the metric system to measure things. Metric measurement is used around the world. Here is how different metric measurements compare to customary measurement.

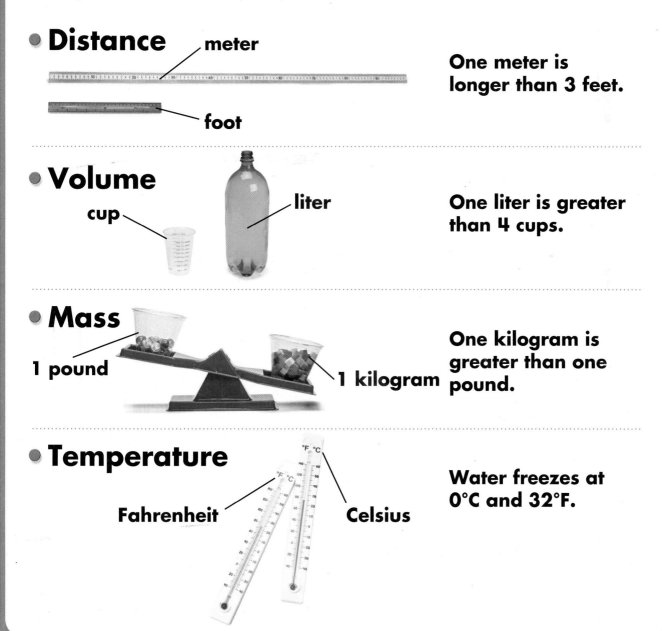

- **Distance**
  meter

  foot

  One meter is longer than 3 feet.

- **Volume**
  cup

  liter

  One liter is greater than 4 cups.

- **Mass**
  1 pound

  1 kilogram

  One kilogram is greater than one pound.

- **Temperature**
  Fahrenheit

  Celsius

  Water freezes at 0°C and 32°F.

Glossary

The glossary uses letters and signs to show how words are pronounced. The mark′ is placed after a syllable with a primary or heavy accent. The mark ′ is placed after a syllable with a secondary or lighter accent.

To hear these words pronounced, listen to the AudioText CD.

A

alike (ə līk′) How things are the same. The two foxes look **alike**. (pages 5, 53, 213)

antennae (an ten′ē) Feelers that help some animals know what is around them. **Antennae** help the crab feel, smell, and taste. (page 56)

Antennae

attract (ə trakt′) Attract means to pull toward. Magnets **attract** some objects. (page 256)

B

battery (bat′ər ē) Something that stores energy. The toy robot uses a **battery** to move. (page 293)

C

camouflage (kam′ə fläzh) A color or shape that makes an animal or plant hard to see. **Camouflage** helps the rabbit stay safe in its environment. (page 62)

cause (kȯz) Why something happens. Taking out the bottom block can cause the tower to fall. (pages 245, 254)

clay (klā) A soft part of soil that looks like mud, is sticky when wet, and is hard when dry. The **clay** felt sticky when Tanya touched it. (page 156)

cloud (kloud) A form in the air made of many tiny drops of water or pieces of ice when water vapor cools. We watched the fluffy, white **clouds** float overhead. (page 186)

 D

desert (dez′ərt) A desert is a very dry habitat that gets little rain. Many **deserts** are hot during the day. (page 38)

different (dif′ər ənt) How things are not the same. The dogs are different colors. (pages 5, 53, 96, 213)

dissolve (di zolv′) To spread throughout a liquid. Salt will **dissolve** in water. (page 225)

draw conclusions

(drȯ kən klü′zhənz) When you decide something about what you see or read. You can **draw** a **conclusion** about what the shark will eat. (pages 117, 277)

E

effect (ə fekt′) What happens. The **effect** of pulling out the bottom block was that the blocks fell down. (pages 245, 254)

electricity (i lek′tris′ə tē) Makes things work. The streetlight uses **electricity** to shine. (page 290)

energy (en′ər jē) Something that can change things. Sunlight is a form of **energy** from the Sun. (page 282)

erosion (i rō′zhən) Happens when wind or water moves rocks and soil from one place to another. **Erosion** washed away the soil near the stream. (page 158)

evaporate (i vap′ə rāt′) To change from a liquid to a gas. The water on the ground quickly **evaporated** when the Sun came out. (page 228)

F

flower (flou′ər) The part of a plant that makes seeds. Our garden has many colorful **flowers**. (page 69)

food chain (füd chān) The way food passes from one living thing to another. All living things are connected through **food chains.** (page 125)

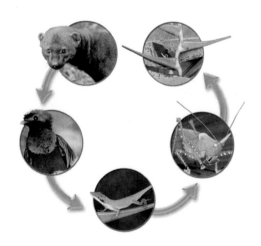

force (fôrs) A push or pull that makes objects move. The children used **force** to move the sled. (page 247)

forest (fôr′ist) A habitat with many trees and other types of plants. Many animals live in the **forest**. (page 31)

fuel (fyü′əl) Anything that is burned to make heat or power. People use gasoline as a **fuel** for cars. (page 290)

G

gas (gas) A kind of matter that can change size and shape. The bubbles are full of **gas**. (page 221)

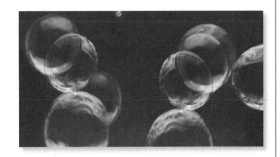

gravity (grav′ə tē) A force that pulls things toward the ground. **Gravity** pulls falling leaves toward the ground. (page 247)

H

habitat (hab′ə tat) A place where plants and animals live. A deer lives in a forest **habitat**. (page 31)

heat (hēt) Moves from warmer places and objects to cooler places and objects. The **heat** from the campfire kept us warm. (page 279)

humus (hyü′ məs) A nonliving material made up of parts of living things that have died. Grandmother adds **humus** to the soil to help her plants grow. (page 156)

important details (im pôrt′nt di tālz′) Pictures and words that tell you about something. We looked for **important details** in the book we were reading. (pages 149, 317)

inclined plane (in klīnd′ plān) A simple machine that is high at one end and low at the other. It helps move things up and down. The builders used an **inclined plane** to help move the wood. (page 359)

larva (lär′və) A young insect that has a different shape from the adult. A butterfly **larva** is called a caterpillar. (page 92)

leaf (lēf) A part of a plant that makes food for the plant. A **leaf** fell from the rose bush. (page 69)

lever (lev′ər) A simple machine that can be used to lift something. Denny used a **lever** to lift the nail out. (page 358)

life cycle (līf sī′kəl) The changes that take place as a plant or an animal grows and changes. The **life cycle** of a frog includes an egg, a tadpole, and a grown frog. (page 90)

liquid (lik′wid) Matter that takes the shape of its container. Water is a **liquid**. (page 220)

living (liv′ing) Things that are alive and can grow and change. The butterfly is a **living** thing. (page 7)

magnet (mag′nit) An object that attracts some kinds of metal. A **magnet** can pull an object made of iron without touching it. (pages 256, 258)

marsh (märsh) A wetland habitat. Many different plants and animals live in a **marsh**. (page 126)

mass (mas) Amount of matter in an object. Everything made of matter has **mass**. (page 215)

matter (mat′er) Anything that takes up space. Everything around you is made of **matter**. (page 215)

mineral (min′ər əl) A nonliving material that can be found in rocks and soil. Copper is a **mineral**. (page 164)

Moon (mün) An object in the sky that moves around Earth. The **Moon** was shining brightly in the night sky. (page 326)

natural resource (nach′ər əl ri sôrs′) A useful thing that comes from nature. Rocks are a **natural resource**. (page 155)

nonliving (non liv′ing) Things that are not alive, don't grow, and don't change on their own. Tables and chairs are **nonliving** things. (page 14)

ocean (ō′shən) A large, deep habitat that has salt water. Some fish live in an **ocean** habitat. (page 36)

oxygen (ok′sə jən) A gas in the air that plants and animals need to live. Most living things need **oxygen** to live. (page 121)

planet (plan′it) A large body of matter that moves around the Sun. Earth is one of the nine **planets**. (page 324)

pole (pōl) At the end of some magnets. The north **pole** of one magnet will attract the south **pole** of another magnet. (page 256)

predict (pri dikt′) To make a guess from what you already know. See the clouds high in the sky. What do you **predict** the weather will be like? (page 181)

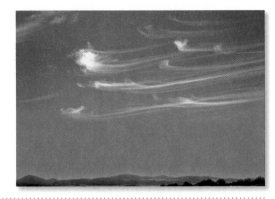

pulley (pùl′ē) A simple machine that uses a wheel and rope to move things up and down. The workers used a **pulley** to move the wood. (page 358)

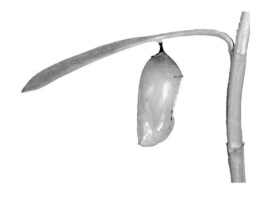

pupa (pyü′pə) The step after larva in some insects' life cycle. The hard covering of the **pupa** protects the caterpillar while it changes into a butterfly. (page 92)

R

rain forest (rān fôr′ist) A habitat that gets a lot of rain. Plants with large green leaves grow in the **rain forest**. (page 122)

repel (ri pel′) To push away. The north poles of two magnets placed together will **repel** each other. (page 257)

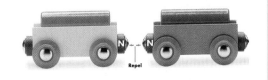

rocks (roks) Nonliving things that come from Earth. José collects **rocks**. (page 154)

root (rüt) Part of a plant that holds the plant in place and takes in water for the plant. We covered the **roots** of the rose plant with soil. (page 68)

rotation (rō tā′shən) The act of turning around and around. Earth's **rotation** causes day and night. (page 322)

S

sand (sand) Tiny pieces of broken rock. We made castles of **sand** at the beach. (page 154)

screw (skrü) A simple machine used to hold things together. A **screw** was used to keep the two wooden boards together. (page 358)

season (sē′zn) One of the four parts of the year. Winter is my favorite **season**. (page 192)

seed coat (sēd kōt) The protective shell that covers and protects a seed. The **seed coat** breaks open as the plant begins to grow. (page 98)

seedling (sēd′ling) A very young plant. Rafiq planted the **seedling** in his yard. (page 98)

shadow (shad′ō) A dark shape made when something blocks light. The doll made a **shadow** on the floor. (page 286)

shelter (shel′tər) A safe place for animals and people. This wolf pup uses an old log for **shelter**. (page 12)

simple machine (sim′pəl mə shēn′) A tool with few or no moving parts that does work. The wheel and axle of this wheelbarrow is a **simple machine**. (page 356)

sleet (slēt) Sleet is frozen rain. **Sleet** made the roads very slippery. (page 189)

solid (sol′id) A kind of matter that takes up space and has its own shape. A wooden block is a **solid**. (page 218)

speed (spēd) How quickly or slowly something moves. The car moved at a very fast **speed**. (page 250)

star (stär) A big ball of hot gas. **Stars** shine brightly in the night sky. (pages 319, 324)

stem (stem) The part of a plant that carries water to the leaves. The rose's **stem** has sharp thorns. (page 68)

Sun (sun) A big ball of hot gas that makes the day sky bright. The light from the **Sun** warms the Earth. (page 319)

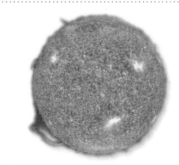

 T

tadpole (tad'pōl') A very young frog. Rosie caught **tadpoles** in the pond. (page 87)

technology (tek nol′ə jē) The use of scientific knowledge to solve problems. A computer is a machine that uses **technology**. (page 343)

telescope (tel′ə skōp) Makes things that are far away look closer and brighter. We use a **telescope** to look at the stars in the sky. (page 324)

temperature (tem′per ə chər) How hot or cold something is. The **temperature** can be very hot in the desert. (page 184)

thermometer (thər mom′ə tər) A tool that measures temperature. We looked at the **thermometer** to see how cold it was outside. (page 184)

vibrate (vī′brāt) To move back and forth very fast. The banjo strings **vibrate** to make sounds. (page 260)

water vapor (wȯ′tər vā′pər) A form of water in the air. You cannot see **water vapor**. (page 186)

weather (weŦH′ ər) What it is like outside. I like to make snowmen when the **weather** outside is cold and snowy. (page 183)

weathering (weŦH′ər ing) The breaking apart and changing of rocks. **Weathering** can change the shape, size, and color of rocks. (page 158)

wedge (wej) A simple machine used to push things apart. The farmer used a shovel as a **wedge** to break up the soil. (page 356)

wetland (wet′land′) A habitat that is covered with water. Tanya saw a bullfrog when she visited the **wetland** near her home. (page 34)

wheel and axle (hwēl and ak′səl) A simple machine used to move things. A wheelbarrow has a **wheel and axle**. (page 356)

Index

This index lists the pages on which topics appear in this book. Page number after a *p* refer to a photograph or drawing.

Credits

Text

"The Frog on the Log" by Ilo Orleans from *Read-Aloud Rhymes for the Very Young* selected by Jack Prelutsky. Copyright ©1986 by Alfred A. Knopf.

"Wind" from *Some Folks Like Cats and Other Poems* by Ivy O. Eastwick. Reprinted by permission of Boyds Mills Press.

"Merry-Go-Round" from *I Like Machinery* by Dorothy Baruch.

"Taking Off" from *Very Young Verses*, edited by Barbara Peck Geismer and Antoinette Brown Suter. Copyright ©1945 by Houghton Mifflin company; Copyright ©Renewed 1972 by Barbara P. Geismer and Antoinette Brown Suter. Reprinted by permission of Houghton Mifflin Company. All Rights Reserved.

Illustrations

31-32, 34, 36, 38 Robert Hynes; 108-109 Cheryl Mendenhall; 322 Henk Dawson.

Photographs

Every effort has been made to secure permission and provide appropriate credit for photographic material. The publisher deeply regrets any omission and pledges to correct errors called to its attention in subsequent editions.

Unless otherwise acknowledged, all photographs are the property of Scott Foresman, a division of Pearson Education.

Photo locators denoted as follows: Top (T), Center (C), Bottom (B), Left (L), Right (R), Background (Bkgd).

Cover: (C) ©Tui De Roy/Minden Pictures, (Bkgd) ©Tim Davis/Corbis, (BL) Getty Images.

Front Matter: ii ©DK Images; iii (TR, B) ©DK Images; v ©DK Images; vi (B) ©DK Images, (CL) Corbis; vii Getty Images; viii (CL) Digital Vision, (BC) ©DK Images; ix (CR) ©Michael and Patricia Fogden/Corbis, (B) ©DK Images; x (TL, CL, B) ©Michael & Patricia Fogden/Corbis, (BR) ©Rick and Nora Bowers/Visuals Unlimited; xii (CL) ©Richard Price/Getty Images, (CL) ©Thomas Kitchin/Tom Stack & Associates, Inc.; xiii (CR) Stephen Oliver/©DK Images, (CR) Getty Images; xiv (CL) Getty Images, (B) ©DK Images; xv ©Frank Siteman/PhotoEdit; xvi ©Stone/Getty Images; xvii Courtesy of the London Toy and Model Museum/Paddington, London/©DK Images; xviii (CL) NASA Image Exchange, (CL) ©Roger Ressmeyer/Corbis; xix ©Lowell Georgia/Corbis; xx ©DK Images; xxii ©Douglas Faulkner/Photo Researchers, Inc.; xxiii ©William Harrigan/Lonely Planet Images; xxiv ©William Harrigan/Lonely Planet Images; xxv (BC) ©John Pontier/Animals Animals/Earth Scenes, (TR) ©Ames/NASA; xxix ©Ed Bock/Corbis; xxxi ©Little Blue Wolf Productions/Corbis; xxxii ©Andy Crawford/DK Images.

Unit A: Divider: ©Wayne R. Bilenduke/Getty Images; 1 (C) ©Sumio Harada/Minden Pictures, (TR) ©Royalty-Free/Corbis; 2 (B) Corbis, (T) ©Pat O'Hara/Corbis; 3 Mary Kate Denny/PhotoEdit; 5 (Bkgd) ©Pat O'Hara/Corbis, (C) ©Royalty-Free/Corbis, (TR) ©DK Images; 6 ©Pat O'Hara/Corbis; 7 (BR) ©Darrell Gulin/Corbis, (TR) ©DK Images; 8 (TR) ©Photowood, Inc./Corbis, (TL) Getty Images; 9 (TL) ©Manoj Shah/Animals Animals/Earth Scenes, (BR) ©J. & B. Photographers/Animals Animals/Earth Scenes; 10 (BL) ©Roy Morsch/Corbis, (TL) Digital Vision; 11 ©Guy Edwardes/Getty Images; 12 (BL) ©Darrell Gulin/Corbis, (C) Corbis, (TL) ©DK Images; 13 ©Dan Guravich/Corbis; 14 ©Mary Kate Denny/PhotoEdit; 16 (TL, C) ©DK Images; 17 Brand X Pictures; 22 (TC) ©Manoj Shah/Animals Animals/Earth Scenes, (B) ©J. & B. Photographers/Animals Animals/Earth Scenes; 23 (TR) ©Darrell Gulin/Corbis, (CL, C) ©DK Images; 24 (TL) Alan Schroeder/Courtesy of Sonia Ortega, (B) ©John Bova/Photo Researchers, Inc.; **Chapter 2:** 25 (C) Getty Images, (TR) ©Stephen Dalton/Photo Researchers, Inc.; 26 (C) ©W. Perry Conway/Corbis, (BL) ©Daniel J. Cox/Natural Exposures, (BR) ©David Samuel Robbins/Corbis; 27 (BR) ©Yva Momatiuk/John Eastcott/Minden Pictures, (BL) Digital Vision; 29 (Bkgd) ©W. Perry Conway/Corbis, (TR, C) ©DK Images; 30 ©W. Perry Conway/Corbis; 31 (BR) ©Taxi/Getty Images, (TR) ©Jeremy Thomas/Natural Visions; 32 (TL) ©Jeremy Thomas/Natural Visions, (BL) ©Jeffrey Lepore/Photo Researchers, Inc., (CR) ©Daniel J. Cox/Natural Exposures; 33 ©Daniel J. Cox/Natural Exposures; 34 (BC) ©Steve Maslowski/Photo Researchers, Inc., (TL) Brand X Pictures; 35 (C) ©David Samuel Robbins/Corbis, (BR) ©Joe McDonald/Corbis, (TR) ©Stone/Getty Images, (CR) Getty Images; 36 (CR) Digital Vision, (TL) ©Stone/Getty Images; 37 (CR) ©Flip Nicklin/Minden Pictures, (TR) Getty Images, (BR) ©Photographer's Choice/Getty Images; 38 (TL) ©Photographer's Choice/Getty Images, (BL) ©DK Images; 39 (BC) ©Yva Momatiuk/John Eastcott/Minden Pictures, (TC) ©Jose Fuste Raga/Corbis; 40 ©Yva Momatiuk/John Eastcott/Minden Pictures, (TR) ©Gerry Ellis/Minden Pictures; 42 (BC) ©Nigel J. Dennis/NHPA Limited, (T) ©Art Wolfe/Stone/Getty Images; 44 (TR, BR) ©Daniel J. Cox/Natural Exposures, (CL) ©David Samuel Robbins/Corbis, (CR) ©Yva Momatiuk/John Eastcott/Minden Pictures, (TR) Digital Vision; 45 (C) ©Robert Lubeck/Animals Animals/Earth Scenes, (TR) Brand X Pictures; 46 NASA; 47 (TR) Getty Images, (CL) ©Porterfield/Chickering/Photo Researchers, Inc., (BR) ©Doug Perrine/DRK Photo; 48 (BC) ©Operation Migration, Inc.; **Chapter 3:** 49 (TL) ©DK Images, (C) ©Michael Patrick O'Neill/NHPA Limited; 50 (BL) ©Richard K. LaVal/Animals Animals/Earth Scenes, (BR) ©T. Kitchin and V. Hurst/NHPA Limited, (C) Digital Vision; 51 (BR) ©Jeff Lepore/Photo Researchers, Inc., (BL) ©J.P. Ferrero/Jacana/Photo Researchers, Inc.; 53 (Bkgd) Digital Vision, (CL) Corel, (CR) ©Lynn Stone/Index Stock Imagery, (TR) ©Helen Williams/Photo Researchers, Inc.; ©54 David Fritts/Stone/Getty Images; 55 (BR) ©Steve Coombs/Photo Researchers, Inc., (TR) Getty Images; 56 (B) ©DK Images, (TL, C) ©B. Jones and M. Shimlock/NHPA Limited; 58 (TL, BL) ©Helen Williams/Photo Researchers, Inc., (BR) ©DK Images; 59 ©Noboru Komine/Photo Researchers, Inc.; 60 (CR) ©Mitsuaki Iwago/Minden Pictures, (TR) Digital Vision, (B) ©S. Purdy Matthews/Stone/Getty Images, (TL) ©Ana Laura Gonzalez/Animals

EM28